Perfume

PAR BREVET DE PERFECTIONNEMENT

EAU DE COLOGNE

DE VOURLOUD

BREVETÉ DE PERFECTIONNEMENT DU GOUVERNEMENT FRANÇAIS,

Approuvée spécialement par la Société Royale de Médecine,
et Fournisseur privilégié de plusieurs Cours étrangères.

Perfume

The Creation and Allure of Classic Fragrances

Susan A. Irvine

CRESCENT BOOKS
NEW YORK • AVENEL

In memory of Desmond Knox-Leet

ACKNOWLEDGMENTS

The author and Haldane Mason would like to thank the following for their help in the preparation of this book. We are very grateful to Bernadette Rendall and Marie-Séverine Hussenot of Chanel, and to Joanna Strachan and Chanel archivist Pierre Bonce, for their unstinting help and support. We would also like to thank Anne Guespin of the Comité Français du Parfum; Andrew Duncan for his scholarly research; Polly Sellar and Lizzie Radford at Vogue for dropping what they were doing to answer frequent questions; Arthur Burnham for his help with Chapter 2 and for letting us adapt his fragrance wheel on page 61; Steve Laczynski, Director of Fragrance Development at Estée Lauder Worldwide for his invaluable help with Chapter 6; Joachim Mensing; Annette Green at the Fragrance Foundation; and Sally Blake for entrusting us with her valuable bottles to photograph and for her perfume wisdom. Martine Uzan of Givaudan-Roure was very helpful in providing pictures, as were Peter Ede of Drom UK; Linda Harman of Quest International; Jean-Pierre Lerouge-Benard at Molinard; Sam Sugiyama at Shiseido; Suzie Meighan at Ogilvy, Adams & Rhinehart; and Kate Moss.

Thanks also to all the PRs who provided perfumes, pictures and information at a moment's notice, including Sophie Peter of Christian Dior; Felicity Bosanquet and Suzy Cunningham at Yves Saint Laurent; Miriam Kelaty and Vicky Murphy at Maurice Douek; Marian Richards at the PR Workshop; Julie Gibson-Jarvie and her team at Riverhouse; Elisabeth Sirot and Barbara Jacquesson at Guerlain; Sarah Griffith and Andrew Rogers at Estée Lauder; Victoria Hennessey and Rowley Weeks at Parfums Givenchy; Astrid Sutton and her team at Astrid Sutton Associates; Marian Scott and Carolyn O'Connor at Revlon; Cassandra Duncan at Lancôme; and Natalie Buckley at Kenneth Green Associates.

The author would also like to thank Deirdre Vine, Editor-in-Chief of *Woman's Journal*, who gave her so many wonderful opportunities to indulge her passion for perfume in the pages of the magazine.

Picture acknowledgments are on page 160.

This 1995 edition is published by Crescent Books, distributed by Random House Value Publishing, Inc., 40 Engelhard Avenue, Avenel, New Jersey 07001.

Random House
New York • Toronto • London • Sydney • Auckland

A CIP catalog record for this book is available from the Library of Congress.

ISBN 0-517-14159-0
10 9 8 7 6 5 4 3 2 1

THIS IS A HALDANE MASON BOOK
Conceived, designed and produced by
Haldane Mason, London

Editor: *Sydney Francis*
Art Director: *Ron Samuels*
Editorial/Production Assistant: *Charles Dixon-Spain*
Picture Researchers: *Jackum Brown, Vicky Walters, Charles Dixon-Spain*
Indexer: *Conan Nicholas*

The right of Susan Irvine to be identified as the author of the text has been asserted by her in accordance with the Copyright Designs and Patents Act 1988.

All illustrations by Debbie Lian Mason, with the exception of those on pages 40–1, 61 and 153 which are by Steven Dew, and page 156 which is reproduced by permission of Rochas. The picture of Kate Moss on pages 127 and 139 is reproduced by kind permission of Kate Moss.

Color reproduction by Imago
Printed in the UK by Jarrold Book Printing, Norwich

CONTENTS

Chapter One

The Mystery of Perfume

The ancients so valued perfumes that they were willing to pay huge prices for ingredients brought thousands of miles by camel and foot, over mountains and deserts, to scent their beds and their temples alike. By comparison, we live in a deodorized world stripped bare of scents. Fragrance no longer plays a central role in our culture. The chaos of smell, that uncontrollable, indefinable emanation from things, disturbs us and we have largely forgotten how to interpret its mysterious language. All that is just starting to change and we are turning to the ancients to learn about fragrance's role as a mind-altering drug and a medicine as well as an aphrodisiac. It's time to tear the last shred of puritanism and prudery from our minds and plunge, nose-first, back into this rich and redolent world of perfumes.

Sacred Scent

'Accompany your prayer with a perfume and your words will reach God transported by an odorous exhalation telling him of your gratitude and devotion,' say the Vedas of ancient India. The word 'perfume' comes from the Latin *per fumum* or 'through smoke', while for the Ancient Greeks the same word meant 'scent' and 'offering to the gods'. The aromatic smoke of incense, smouldering woods, spices and herbs formed the most ancient scents, prerogatives of gods and kings. Two of the gifts brought to Christ were perfumes: myrrh and frankincense. These were precious gifts, equal in commercial value to the third gift, gold, but they were also spiritual offerings, indicative of Christ's holy status.

Arab perfumers from a twelfth-century Persian manuscript selling perfume by weight (*above*). The Arabs preserved the ancient art of perfumery through the Dark Ages and reintroduced techniques like distillation (*below*) to the West. Their perfume culture in the style of the ancients continues to this day.

In previous centuries, the words 'spirit' and 'essence' were used to denote perfume (as in spirit of myrrh or rose essence), indicating its ancient connection with spirituality. Even the modern phrase 'essential oil', describing the fragrant oil of a plant, expresses the idea that the fragrance is the essence of the flower.

Perfume has always been central to magic and religious rituals everywhere. For many ancient societies, breath was sacred, entering the body at birth, leaving it at death. The Bamabara of Mali, like many others, believe that the breath is the soul, communicating with the world by being blown out into it and then sucked back in with its trawl of odours. If breath is the soul of humans, then perfume, the breath of plants, is like the soul of nature, and often the signal of a holy presence on earth. For the ancients, to inhale a perfume was to take into their body the spirit-force of the cosmos.

For the Egyptians, perfume was the sweat of the gods. Myrrh, which looks like frozen droplets, came from Ra, the sun-god, and ben oil (made from moringa nuts) from the eye of Horus. As they prayed, they held incense-burners, called amschirs. These had a long arm with a holder at the end to contain the burning charcoal. It was held in one hand and fed with small pastilles of incense with the other.

As the smoke ascended heavenwards, its spirals turning solid matter into invisible scented breath, it formed a connection between the invisible world of the gods above and the solid world of earth below. At the same time the smoke formed pathways for prayers which, ascending with it, were inhaled by the gods. The Catholic custom of burning a candle as you pray is a vestige of this ancient practice. Each statue of the gods was also anointed with unguents. First, the priest offered incense to the god, then applied its cosmetics before touching its forehead with a drop of perfume with the words: 'Take the oil that comes from the morning offering.'

The Egyptians used several different resins. The oldest was sntr, always depicted with the prefix 'ntr', meaning divine, so that it translates as 'the odour that pleases the gods'. Sntr or sonter came from the terebinth (turpentine) tree. Around 2000 BC this was largely replaced by the mellow balm of frankincense and the austerity of myrrh. The Egyptians imported tons of frankincense and myrrh annually from the mysterious land of Punt, thought to be in modern-day Somalia, and through Jordan and Israel by way of the famous Incense Route from southern Arabia or Saba'a, the land of the Queen of Sheba.

The riches of Arabia Felix ('happy Arabia') were built on its trade in myrrh, frankincense and other scent ingredients. The Arabs tried to shroud the origins of their valuable exports in mystery to keep the business to themselves. Cinnamon, they said, was gathered from the nests of phoenixes or found in remote marshes guarded by winged serpents. Terrible bats tried to snatch out the eyes of anyone who went cassia-picking. Stories like this helped to keep prices high as well.

Mary Magdalene, patron saint of perfumers, anointing Christ's feet with spikenard. This would have been brought overland from India; she used a whole pound of ointment, costing more than US $2,000 in today's money.

The spices imported from Arabia and India by the Egyptians, Assyrians, Babylonians and other Near East cultures were used in cooking as they are today, but their main purposes were to serve as sacerdotal perfumes in religious and funerary rites. Perfumes were among the most important items traded between nations. The exorbitant prices were acceptable because for them perfume was not just a luxury, as it is for us, but a magical substance with the power to bring them closer to divinity.

Burning incense in religious rituals had many purposes. Firstly, the scents were thought to be pleasing to the gods. Secondly, they served as flight-paths for prayers, and Egyptians thought that their very souls would ascend to Ra on the wings of their smoking perfumes. Thirdly, they masked the stench of burnt offerings made to the gods, and later, in Christian churches, were thought to neutralize any evil emanations from bodies buried within the church itself. Many essential oils are indeed purifying, antibacterial and antiseptic.

But the fragrances also served a primary purpose as mind-altering drugs. Incense was burned because of its specific narcotic and sedative qualities. It raised the priests to a higher state of consciousness that they believed brought them into closer communion with the gods. Chemists have analysed frankincense, for example, and found that besides resinous acids it contains four types of terpenes, chemicals which, when inhaled, act on the brain cells like cannabis oil. Because of this,

'A perfume is like an identity card of the spirit,' wrote the modern perfumer Marcel Billot. 'It describes . . . above all, the spirituality of the person who uses it.' In China, incense is sacred and the Chinese climb to the tops of holy mountain like Hua Shan (Flower Mountain) near Xian to enjoy incense and the scents of nature at dawn.

the Ancient Egyptians believed frankincense to be inherently spiritual. It was 'the one that makes god known'.

Other civilizations are less word-orientated than those of the Near East from which our own culture developed. The Maya-Tzotzil of Chiapas in South America do not use perfume as a pathway for prayer, but as a prayer in itself. They burn their incense, copal, as a prayer for health, unaccompanied by any words.

For many cultures, there is a deep connection between scents and other-worldliness. To emit a scent is the furthest an objective reality can go towards dematerializing and becoming pure idea. As Arthur Gell puts it in his

seminal essay *Magic, Perfume, Dream*: 'A mere aroma, in its very lack of substance is more *like* a concept than it is like a "thing".' While we downgrade smell as the lowliest, the grossest of our senses, this abstract nature of the sense of smell was recognized by the ancients. The Latin *sagax* (from which comes our word 'sagacious') means intelligent, and possessed of a keen sense of smell.

For the ancients and many tribal societies today fragrance was the food of the gods. The ancient Greeks fed their gods daily on nectar-sweet perfumes, and the Huichol of South America still burn their incense, copal, today to nourish their divinities. It is

10

interesting that they choose a substance that smells very similar to the incense of the Near East. For many ancient civilizations, a sweet scent was an indication of a holy presence, an idea that continued for centuries in Christianity with the 'odour of sanctity' that was said to accompany many saints, even after death.

At the same time, scent is the symbol *par excellence* of rites of passage. Scent passes under doors, seeps through walls, crosses boundaries. It is uncontainable, the symbol of being between one state and another, a solid state and a dematerialized, disembodied one. Consequently, it is used all over the world by tribal people in 'threshold' ceremonies like initiation into manhood, at marriage, birth or death as part of rituals expressing an individual's passage from one stage of life to another.

In religious rites, perfume is also about transformation. For transubstantiation of the bread and wine to take place in the Catholic ritual, the offerings are purified by incense. Perfume was, and is, also used to bind people together at important ceremonies. For the ancient Egyptians as for the Desana of the Amazon, burning sacred perfumes actualizes their oneness, everyone breathing in the holy emanation together. Certain perfumes do indeed induce a mass response. A sort of communal trance can be brought about by incense infusing into the brain, suppressing the rational and its obsession – control – and allowing the emotive responses of the limbic system to be freed.

The limbic system, seat of smell and emotion, acts directly on the autonomic nervous system. As anthropologist Barbara Lex has pointed out, 'intense stimulation of the

autonomic nervous system retards and prohibits logical reasoning'. Perfume in this role is acting as a magical transformer, the effectiveness of which science is now proving. Different societies use different scents. The Trobriand Islanders use mint, the Umeda ginger, the Catholics balsam or frankincense. Montaigne, the sixteenth-century essayist, wrote: 'I have often noted that [perfumes] cause changes in me, and act on my spirits according to their qualities; which makes me agree with the theory that

the introduction of incense and perfume into churches . . . was for the purpose of raising our spirits, and of exciting and purifying our senses, the better to fit us for contemplation.'

In China, the Taoists utilized the hallucinogenic properties of cannabis. One of their herbals explains that if it is inhaled systematically over time 'one can communicate with the spirits and one's body becomes light'. Other psychoactive aromatics were tossed into their incense-burners as well, which altered their consciousness in a way they interpreted as sacred. 'For those who begin practising the Tao it is not necessary to go into the mountains . . . Some with purifying incense and

An incense burner and devotional joss-sticks sending up their fragrant prayers at the Bamboo Temple in Kunming, China. The early Taoists added hallucinogenic substances to their incense to lighten their spirits and bring them closer to the gods.

sprinkling and sweeping are also able to call down the Perfected Immortals.'

Marijuana was also first used as an incense in the Near East and tobacco leaves, which contain hallucinogenic substances in the raw, were used by early Americans as ritual incense. Certainly the ancients were aware of the narcotic powers of plants. Opium was dissolved in wine and drunk as a medicine, and the Assyrians used cannabis fumigations to dispel grief.

The oriental affinity for the mystery of perfume has inspired many twentieth-century scents, including Enigma. This 1905 ad shows the narcotic and fragrant blue water-lily that the Egyptians loved.

PARFUM
ENIGMA
LUBIN
PARIS

11, RUE ROYALE

One of the earliest perfume-recipes on record is in Exodus. Moses was instructed by God to take the following with him on the Israelites' exit from Egypt: 500 shekels of myrrh, 250 of cinnamon, 250 of sweet-smelling roses, and galbanum, incense and a copious quantity of olive oil so he could blend a sacred perfume 'to be reserved for God alone'. The secrets of making perfumes were closely guarded by the priest castes because of their holy connotations.

Perfume laboratories were attached to temples in Egypt and also in Israel. At En Gedi in Israel, the remains of a temple complex have been found complete with a sixth-century AD perfume laboratory. On the mosaic pavement of the synagogue the following inscription curses anyone who reveals the secrets of the sacred perfumer's art: 'Whosoever shall reveal the secret of the town/To the gentiles – may He whose eyes range over the entire earth/and see the hidden, He shall set His face against that person/and his seed, and shall uproot him from under the heavens/And the entire people say Amen, amen. Selah!'

Similar dire curses invoke horrors on anyone who takes from the temple precinct the recipes for the famous kyphi and other perfumes manufactured at Edfu in Egypt. The apothecaries worked directly under the priests, producing perfumes for the temple and for mummification. The walls of these laboratories were also libraries of stone books, on which precise instructions for making the perfumes were kept. As kyphi was being prepared, the priests read out sacred texts over the vats of boiling oil and flower and spice essences, infusing them with the spirit of the words.

In India, temples were known as 'gandhakuti' or houses of fragrance, and the statues of the gods were washed in a perfume made of musk, sandalwood and agarwood. In Babylon, offerings of perfume were brought yearly to the Tree of Life. The Babylonians believed that the myrrh tree, which at the time also grew on the Babylonian plain, was sacred, and that its bark had split in order for a god, Adoni (Adonis) to be born. For the Ancient Egyptians the first-ever living thing was a gloriously scented flower, the blue water-lily or *Nymphaea caerulea*, often incorrectly identified as the lotus. As it blossomed at the beginning of time, it revealed the Supreme Godhead at its centre. The water-lily opens at dawn and then closes its petals at midday, sinking beneath the water again to rise the next morning. Because of this, it came to symbolize resurrection. The Egyptians adored this flower; lilies were held in the hand and inhaled during banquets, a scene that is often depicted in their murals. Modern analysis has shown that the mildly narcotic and hallucinogenic substances nupharine, nupharidine and nuciferine are released by the plant. Inhalation was backed up by steeping the flowerheads in wine to form a scented potion that would induce reveries and transports.

It would be wrong to present a picture of ancient civilizations as drug-crazed barbarians. The effect of most of these plants was very gentle compared to the sledgehammer effects of modern drugs and the indications are that they were used in a controlled, ritualistic way. But the fact is that the ancients were conscious of the power of many plants to affect the mind and the emotions in a way that we have forgotten, and consequently they were able to benefit from this as they chose.

Modern aromatherapy and aromachology are now backing up much of what the ancients believed

A terracotta incense-burner from the ancient Mayan civilization of Mexico. The main priest figure may represent the sun god. He rests his foot on a turtle's shell from which emerges the god of the underworld.

about the mind-altering effects of essential oils. Some stimulate, others relieve anxieties, others can lift our mood when we are feeling low. The Tibetan monk who lights a stick of sandalwood incense before meditating is benefiting from its age-old power to enhance the mind's capacity to empty itself. As Muhammad says in the Koran: 'Perfumes are foods that reawaken the spirit, and the spirit is the camel on which man rides and has himself carried.'

The Perfumed Pharmacy

'A perfume is always a medicine' is an ancient Chinese saying. The Chinese were prolific users of *hsiang yao* or aromatic medicines, as were the Arabs and Persians. Their oldest pharmacopoeia, *The Book of Medicines*, contains hundreds of perfume preparations to be used in healing. Where we compartmentalize, the ancients were holistic. They saw the healing, transcendent and aphrodisiac qualities of perfume as different aspects of one unifying plant energy. Kyphi, the celebrated perfume of the ancient Egyptians, was burned at sundown in the temples of the sun-god, Ra, but its aromatherapeutic properties were also recognized. Pliny wrote that it 'lulled one to sleep, allayed anxieties and brightened dreams'. At the same time, it had a sensual effect, being 'made of those things that delight most in the night'.

Many non-Western cultures retain this holistic attitude to perfumes. For example, in North Africa, women wear scented necklaces blended from ambergris, cloves, agarwood, rose petals, saffron and nutmeg, ground to a very fine powder and made into a paste with a little oil of jasmine or rose. Hardened, these can be formed into beads, which in contact with the warmth of the skin serve two functions: to keep bad spirits at bay, and to attract the opposite sex. Many of the ingredients in these scent amulets are also used in North African medicine.

For the ancient Egyptians, perfumes were 'the mucus of life' and, as such, they were essential in the ritual of embalming the dead. They believed in

The four main perfumes of the Hebrews (*clockwise from top left*): cinnamon, balm of Judea (now extinct) being collected from cut bark, nard and valerian.

the transmigration of the soul. After death, the soul entered the bodies of land, water and then air animals before returning to its original human form. It was therefore paramount that the body still be there when the soul returned to reclaim it.

14

The soul of the dead person also used the incense smoke as a stairway to heaven: 'A stairway to the sky is set up for me that I may ascend on it.' By a strange turn of fate, these highly perfumed corpses later came back into use as a perfume ingredient called mummiya. The Greeks and early Arabs used the resin-soaked mummies, finely powdered, in their perfumes.

Of course, perfumes were also medicines for the living, each having a reputation for different healing purposes: myrrh was used especially in healing wounds, spikenard combated epilepsy, hysteria and other convulsions, and megaleion, a famous ancient Greek perfume, was used to reduce inflammation. Because of its analgesic and psychoactive properties, myrrh was also a painkiller; dissolved in wine, it was offered to Christ before his crucifixion. Modern aromatherapy is teaching us that many essential oils do indeed have medicinal qualities.

Fumigations were used to get rid of the 'demons of disease' by many ancient civilizations. Until modern times, disease was thought to be caused by miasmas or evil vapours released from the earth into the air. For example, the word 'malaria' comes from the Italian for 'bad air' – *mal airia*. The logical way to combat bad air was to drive it off with a shield of good air,

and consequently, resins, spices and woods were burned to do this. Hippocrates saved Athens from the plague by burning huge bonfires of aromatic woods in the streets, and as late as the eighteenth century, fires of juniper wood were burned in the streets of Paris to ward off infections.

As well as being part of the physical pharmacopoeia, perfume was the ultimate brainfood. Scents were used to treat melancholy, and to nourish the spirit, a function which the ancients took seriously. As Galen, the famous Greek physician, said, 'He who has two cakes of bread, let him dispose of one of them for some flowers of the narcissus; for bread is the food of the body and the narcissus is the food of the soul.'

Shi-Che, the Chinese goddess of perfume.

Perfumes, toiletries and medicines were linked in the ancient world and are still sold side-by-side today. Many companies like Shiseido in Japan who make cosmetics and scents also produce pharmaceuticals and hygiene products like this toothpaste.

Perfume in Everyday Ancient Life

Do you ever wonder what the sun *smells* like? The Desana people of Colombia say it has the smell of honey, while the ancient Greeks assigned it the hot smell of spices.

The Japanese once divided up the day with incense-clocks, burning a different incense every hour, while the Andaman Islanders divide the year with a perfume calendar. Each period of the year is named for the fragrant flower in bloom at the time. When a young girl begins to menstruate, which they call her 'blossoming time', she takes on the name of the current bloom. She keeps this name until she bears her 'first fruit' or first child, when she reverts to her birth name.

Perhaps the first deliberate use of scent was to help us kill. Neanderthal man rubbed his body with the fur of his prey to enable him to creep closer in the hunt. Later, perfumes were used to kill in more sophisticated ways. An improbable assassination attempt was made on Alexander the Great by throwing a dusky maiden into his arms, her breath scented with a deadly poison.

Ancient civilizations revelled in scent the way we do in images and sounds. The Chinese tucked sachets of perfumed powders into their sleeves, had perfume-burners and joss sticks smouldering in every room, and kept the prunings of aromatic tree barks in their laundry. They impregnated paper strips with

A Grecian terracotta perfume vase depicting a woman beautifying herself with perfumes and cosmetics.

LE LIVRE DES PARFUMS   CHAP V.

LA TOILETTE D'APRES UN VASE GREC

perfume, tearing bits off to scent themselves and guests leaving banquets were given jasmine balls to clear their heads after drinking wine. At one point, even Chinese money was printed on silk and perfumed.

In Egypt as in ancient China, hygiene was of prime importance. Egyptians bathed once a day, sometimes several times, and afterwards anointed themselves with scented oils or unguents. They also used the most bizarre scent accessory, a habit which continued into the early twentieth century among some Egyptian Bedouin tribes. At banquets, guests were presented with cones of unguent, a mixture of ox fat and aromatics, that were worn like crowns attached by a little spike sticking out of their wigs.

Rich Romans similarly were not content that things should look good – they had to smell good too. They slept on mattresses stuffed with roses, released doves drenched in different scents to flutter over guests at banquets, and strewed the floors of their bridal chambers with snowdrifts of rose petals. Their daily bath involved a visit to the unctuarium, or anointing room, where slaves massaged them with oils: rhodium, which smelt of roses, melinum, of quinces, or narcissum, of narcissus.

In the United Arab Emirates, where the culture of perfume has remained largely unchanged since

antiquity, the ancient Greek practice of scenting different parts of the body with different perfumes is still continued. After a meal, guests are offered a round of perfumes where Westerners might offer chocolates. Even water is perfumed and purified with frankincense smoke. The Arabs still retain a holistic approach to their native scents – frankincense is also used as a stomach medicine and gum-cleanser, for example. They cense their houses and mosques once a week to purify them of evil. They believe that a smelly, dirty body is vulnerable to evil while a scented person is surrounded by angels. Frankincense is thought to be the most beneficial for attracting angels.

Western commercial perfumes are diluted in alcohol, but the Arabs retain the ancient method of dissolving perfumes in oil, which fixes the scents better so they last longer. Pure alcohol was unknown to the ancients. They dissolved some perfumes in wine, but

A 1,500-year-old wall-painting shows three Egyptian women at a banquet wearing cones of scented unguent. The heat would melt the cones, sending cooling runnels of scent trickling through their ringlets and down their bodies. One of them inhales the mildly narcotic scent of a blue water-lily.

most of them in fat or oils. They had several methods of extracting the essences from flowers. The oldest was pressing, where the plants were placed in a linen cloth with a loop at either end and simply wrung out. They also macerated plants in oil and fat, sometimes boiling it for long periods. A third method was a crude means of distillation, later lost in the West but preserved by the Arabs, who reintroduced it to Europe.

Even the streets of the ancients were redolent with rich aromas. Not all were pleasant. Excrement, rotting food and the unclean bodies of the very poor mingled with the heavenly smells of incense and flower garlands. In some places the very walls of the buildings were scented. Pliny wrote about the temple at Elis where the plaster had been mixed with milk and saffron. Later, some Arab mosques had musk mixed with the mortar so that a divine aura of perfume would exude from the building in the heat of the sun.

Aphrodisia

Perfumes were divine, but they were also sensual. Muslim men look forward to a paradise peopled by beautiful houris whose only purpose is to fulfil their desires and whose bodies are made entirely of musk. Assyrian kings enjoyed maidens whose bodies had first been macerated for twelve months in special perfume-baths (six months in myrrh and six in labdanum or

'In summertime the beautiful women of the court perfume their breasts with sandal oil, their hair with jasmine oil, and the rest of their bodies with rose oil. They are ready for love.' (From *The Seasons* by Kildasa).

bdellium). The Chinese were even more exquisite. Courtesans were fed on bland foods flavoured with musk, so that when their skin was stroked in the act of love their heated bodies sweated pure perfume.

In many languages, the word for 'to kiss' and 'to smell' is the same. Anthropologists have posited that kissing is really an extended process of amorously tasting and smelling your lover. The ancients revelled in the perfume of kisses. The Roman poet Martial describes his boy-lover's kisses as: 'Breath of balm from phials of yesterday, of the last effluence that falls from a curving jet of saffron; perfume of apples ripening in their winter chest, of fields lavish with the leafage of spring; of Augusta's silken robes from Palatine presses, of amber warmed by a maiden's hand, of a garden that strays therein Sicilian bees; the scent of Cosmus' alabaster boxes, and of the altar of the gods; of a chaplet fallen but now from a rich man's locks – why should I speak of each? Not enough are they; mix them all; such is the fragrance of my boy's kisses at morn.'

Cosmus was a famous Roman perfumer; Megallus was a Greek, creator of the famous megaleion, a blend of rush, reed, cassia, resins, ben nut oil and balsam. Many other perfumes came from Crete, or, above all, from Egypt, rated the land of perfumes *par excellence*. Perfumes like these served, as they do today, as love-gifts. In both the *Kama Sutra* of India and *The Perfumed Garden* of Arabia, instructions are given on how perfumes can fan the flames of love.

A woman of the harem pouring on scented oils after the bath, as imagined by a European Orientalist. Above the bath, a putto supports a phalanx of caskets, vases and bottles for unguents and oils. For Victorians the East symbolized sensual abandonment.

Scent was essential to sex. The Song of Solomon is one long hymn of praise to its erotic powers: 'An enclosed garden are you, my sister, my bride, a sealed source of fragrance. Your plants, an orchard of pomegranates with fragrant fruits and flowers.' Cleopatra welcomed Antony to a bedroom inches deep in rose petals and women fumigated their vulvas with myrrh-smoke to scent and purify them. One animal ingredient that was considered highly sexy by the ancients was onycha, the perculum of a species of sea-snail (*Unguis odoratus*). It is still crushed to a powder and mixed with frankincense, cinnamon and cloves by Sudanese women.

Like animals on heat, lovelorn Greeks left tributes of scent-spoors for their loved ones. Lucretius writes of 'the tearful lover [who] smothers the threshold with flowers and garlands

and anoints the haughty doorposts with marjoram'. The scents of a fresh human body were also treasured. One ancient custom that survived into Elizabethan times was that of love-apples. A peeled apple was tucked into the armpit for a day, then presented to a lover. Scented as it was with sexual excretions from the apocrine glands, and the sweetness of the apple, it acted as a persuasive aphrodisiac.

The ancients snuffed their lovers with a full-blooded sensuality that we deny ourselves. 'She passed close by and I did not glimpse her face/But her scented trail has kindled my desire/With voluptuous images which I should like to fulfil with her' (Ti Fun, Tang Dynasty). Perhaps in our modern world saturated with worn pictorial representations of sex, it is time to turn to this more tantalizing path of seduction.

Perfume in Europe

The early Christians reacted against the excesses of the Roman Empire by adopting an ascetic approach to the senses. The culture of perfume, therefore, went underground in the West for almost a thousand years, until the Middle Ages, when crusaders returning from the aromatic Middle East gradually reintroduced customs and scents that had been lost.

At first, the capital of perfumery in Europe was Venice. It was here that the Venetian merchants unloaded their ships of spices, resins, musk, silks and rosewater from Arabia, India, Egypt and China. Perfumers abounded in the city, and also in Florence. In 1573 Edward de Vere, Earl of Oxford, brought back from his travels in Italy 'perfumed gloves, sweet bags, and other plesant things' which delighted the Elizabethan court.

Although perfume-sellers are recorded in Paris as early as 1190, it was Catherine de Medici who made Paris the fashionable city of perfume when she came to France in 1533 to marry Henri II. With her came René, her perfumer, who established his famous shop on the Pont au Change, bizarrely decorated with ibises and mummies from Egypt as well as deathsheads, while a stuffed crocodile hung from the ceiling. Two silver lamps filled with perfumed oil cast an eerie yellow glow over the room and, upstairs, all the alchemists' paraphernalia of alembics, crucibles and retorts were contained in a small

A fifteenth-century monk buys incense from a perfume merchant.

'The Perfumer's Dress' (*opposite*), an engraving from the end of the seventeenth century, advertises a perfumer's wares. On his head is a perfume burner, while his shoulders sport scented fans; one hand holds washballs, the other, glove leather, while his tray holds essences, Naples soaps and toilet waters. The big jar in the middle contains breath pastilles and burning pastilles. Next to it is a glove.

chamber. It was rumoured to be Catherine's alchemist, Cosimo Ruggiero, who brewed poisonous perfumes including the scented gloves that killed Jeanne d'Albret, Henri II's mistress.

In Renaissance Europe, people were as status-conscious about their gloves as we might be about watches. However, the urine used to cure the skins left its malodorous mark on the leather, so gloves were heavily scented to disguise this. Grasse, a small town in the south of France known as a tanning centre, also had a superb microclimate that encouraged a profusion of wild herbs and flowers to grow all over the slopes of the maritime alps that surround it. The peasants would strap their crude alembics or stills to a donkey and wander the hills, distilling on the spot bunches of lavender, thyme, rose and orange blossom. They sold the essences to apothecaries and alchemists, and increasingly to the glovemakers.

Gradually a guild of glovemaker-perfumers grew up in the area, utilizing the local flora but also importing perfumes from further afield, and selling not only perfumed gloves but perfumes of all kinds. Grasse developed into the centre of the Western perfumery industry, and by the eighteenth century when the leather business declined, the glovemaker-perfumers dropped the gloves and evolved into perfumers exclusively.

Habit de Parfumeur

Fragrance is still sold in pharmacies today, and in previous centuries it was apothecaries who dispensed perfumes along with their remedies. Many monasteries had laboratories where monk-apothecaries made perfumes, potions blessed by bishops, soaps, ointments and unguents, miraculous elixirs and sachets of pulverized iris root for perfuming linen. One of these, the Officina Profumo-Farmaceutica di Santa Maria Novella, survives from 1612, housed in a magnificent vaulted room at the back of the monastery. Here, you can buy 'liquori' like Elixir

An eighteenth-century morning toilette could take hours of perfuming, patching and pasting. Here the mistress of the house is about to have her hair powdered while a servant brings a perfume burner.

dolce di China and tincture of myrrh for cleansing the mouth, alongside the most fascinating perfumes and colognes: Peau d'Espagne cologne, a famous centuries-old blend once used for scenting Spanish leather, Heliotrope and Ambergris waters, Snow Cream for moisturizing the skin, and the only pot-pourri worth having in the world.

By the seventeeth century, most English families of note also had their own distilling-rooms where they distilled and macerated perfumes and herbal remedies. Directing the running of the still-room was one of the most important duties of the mistress of a household. Scents were used liberally as medicines, as household deodorants and on the person. Floors were strewn with rushes (sweet flag), May blossom, lavender and meadowsweet (Elizabeth I's favourite), while 'perfume-cakes' were set to smoulder on the embers to sweeten the air of a room. In large households there were servants whose job was purely to fumigate musty rooms and sour clothes. In his *Calendar of Gardening* of 1661, Stevenson writes: 'Be sure every morning to perfume the house with angelica seeds, burnt in a fire-pan or chafing dish of coales.' These fumigations were thought to ward off airborne illnesses as well (many essential oils are, in fact, powerful germicides).

Pomanders composed of ambergris and benzoin were hung from belts and tiny ones were strung on chains and worn as necklaces, both as fragrances and to ward off olfactory evils. Gradually, everything became scented, from pet dogs, snuff and tobacco to precious stones. Heavy scents were favoured on the whole, rich in spices, musk and ambergris. Until the very end of the eighteenth century, Europeans themselves smelt strongly.

Le Matin

Quoy que je sois belle et charmante   Il faut pour me rendre contente
N'espargne rien icy en mes ajustements   que je plaise a tous mes amants
se vend a Paris chez P. Valran au coin de la rue de Savoye proche les grands Augustins

Washing was seen as potentially dangerous, not to be undertaken frequently. Medical opinion held that the best protection against illnesses was to smell strongly yourself, warding off plague-ridden miasmas with your own potent smell-shield of body odour strengthened with animal scents of musk, ambergris and civet.

Plague-waters were also used to keep diseases at bay. Eau d'Hongrie or Hungary Water, made for the Queen of Hungary around 1370, was the first of these. It was also said that she was miraculously rejuvenated by using it, receiving a marriage proposal from the King of Poland in her seventies. Oleum Philosophorum and Acqua Perlata were other cure-alls, but the most famous was Eau de Cologne, still made under the name of 4711.

Eau de Cologne is a blend of attar of neroli with other orange oils, together with rosemary and bergamot. It was originally known as Acqua Admirabilis, and was brought from Italy to Cologne in Germany in 1694 by Giovanni Paolo de Feminis. De Feminis spread the story that the recipe had been given him by a monk whose life he saved. It is more likely that it was developed by English military doctors in India to combat dysentery.

The Feminis family made a large fortune from their panacea, and the recipe then passed to the Farina brothers, who marketed it successfully with an advertisement that promised it to be 'a miraculous antidote against poisons of all kinds, and an outstanding prohylactic against plague', plus a dispeller of 'all hardened, tough slime caused by the heat of unplesant winds'.

In the seventeenth century, Louis XIV of France was dubbed 'the sweetest-smelling monarch that had

Originally a panacea, Eau de Cologne became popular as an invigorating splash. Napoleon used to crack open a bottle and douse his head and shoulders every morning. Later, in 1853, the wife of Napoleon III commissioned a variation, Eau Impériale, from Guerlain. It is still sold in the original bottle with imperial French bees stamped in gold-dust.

yet been seen', and in his reign the glovemaker-perfumers gained additional patents and favours. One of his favourite perfumes was Acqua Angeli, a mixture of spices, agarwood, jasmine and rosewater with a few grains of musk, and all his shirts were rinsed in it, the way we might use lightly scented fabric conditioner. Under Louis XV the cult of perfumes became even more lavish, with courtiers ordered to wear a different scent each day, so that Versailles became known as 'la cour parfumée'. At Choisy, the king's mistress, Madame de Pompadour, spent more on perfume in her household expenses than anything else: half a million livres a year. By the eighteenth century, the French court was consuming almost as much perfume as the sensual citizens of ancient Rome.

In London, a Minorcan, Juan Floris, set up shop in Jermyn Street in 1730. After the Farmacia de Santa Maria Novella in Florence, Floris is the oldest perfumers still in existence, replete with royal warrants from succeeding British courts. It was celebrated for its English 'livinder water' and rose scents, many of which are still made to the original recipes. Yardley, which began in 1770 as bucklers, was selling lavender grown in Norfolk and macerated in bear grease for dressing men's hair by 1817. By the end of the nineteenth century it was the largest manufacturer of lavender products in the world, and it still sells delicate English lavender water today.

Although Marie-Antoinette started a fashion for lighter, more innocent scents like violet and rose, the predominant trend throughout the eighteenth century was a continuation of the odalisque aromas of musk, civet, ambergris and spices. But at the end of the century, all this was to change. Our modern horror of smell dates back to this period, when the cult of the individual began.

As communities, we were once bound together by a 'herd odour' just as many animals are. But with the idea of individual democratic rights came the right to pure, clean air, unflavoured by the strong smells of other people. The common, binding herd odour was replaced by the idea of 'personal space'. This personal space is like spiritual, olfactory property – not to be invaded by the smells of others, unless we invite them into it.

The nineteenth century was the era of sanitation and deodorization. Until then, European cities had stunk to high heaven. One French reformer, Tournon, described Paris as 'nothing more than a vast cesspool'. But as the air became cleaner and the threshold of sensitivity to smells was raised, so powerful perfumes fell out of favour too. Animal notes, reminiscent of the human body's own effluvia, were frowned on as degenerate. The sense of smell itself was disapproved of. Kant did not include it in his aesthetics, others claimed it was just a leftover from evolution like a residual tail.

The Victorians linked musk with lasciviousness and banned it. Instead, they favoured the pastel tones of toilet waters based on lavender, rosemary, beanflower and strawberry. But even these were not applied directly to the body: too flagrant. Instead, the era of handkerchief perfumes was ushered in. Mittens, slippers and parasols might be lightly freshened; the skin, never. The repression of the passions and the horror of the body evinced in the nineteenth century was most strongly expressed through a denial of smell. 'Misuse of perfumes gives birth to all neuroses,' wrote Dr Rostan as early as

The voluptuous genies of perfume stream blissfully upwards from a Chinese incense-burner in this label from the old Grasseois perfume house of Molinard.

1826. 'Hysteria, hypochondria and melancholia are its most usual effects.'

A depraved libertinage of the nose could even be let loose through the simple act of smelling a flower. The blissful expression on the face of a woman inhaling its fragrance was likened to her expression when making love. Some experts even warned that this dark relationship between woman (the 'animal' sex) and flower could end in orgasm – the ultimate forbidden. At the same time women were equated

Molinard jeune

GRASSE
PARIS

HABANITA

L'EAU DE TOILETTE

with flowers, and the use of 'flower-women' to advertise fragrances was a trend that continues even now with perfumes like Cacharel's Eden.

Scent and sex were irredeemably intertwined. Nothing compared to the odour of a virgin, said to be of marjoram. But once her virginity was lost, a woman's scent was permanently debased by the taint of male sperm. No doubt this had some relevance in that the Victorians, while keen on hygiene, rarely washed their genitalia because of the embarrassment of touching or seeing them. 'Close your eyes until you have completed the operation,' Madame de Celnart instructed her readers in her etiquette manual.

As for musk itself, it became positively satanic, with the power to unleash repressed sexuality and shatter social norms. In Edmond de Goncourt's novel *Chérie*, the heroine procures some musk which she sniffs in bed like some illicit drug, leading to an orgasm. Divine retribution decrees that she die a virgin, without having known the real smell of a man (very like musk).

Victorians wanted their women to be as sweet and innocent as flowers, especially the shy, retiring violet, which was used for soaps, as in this label, as well as for toilet waters, handkerchief perfumes and for scenting linen.

This distrust of what was now seen as the most debased, the most animal of the senses also heightened the Victorians' feverishness about scent. Men were to protect themselves from the *odor femina* of women, which could strike them helpless like a bewitchment, and as Goethe had written in *Faust*, it was by 'the perfume of incense and roses mixed' with 'fresh living blood' that Paris had driven the palace women mad with hunger for his breath. The repression of smells led to a counter-culture that revelled in them. Freud and the other great sexologists of the late nineteenth century included numerous 'sniffers' in their catalogues of fetishists. Poets like Baudelaire and novelists like Balzac and later, Proust, revelled in describing odours.

History has ignored perfume's sociological role until now, but as Alain Corbin says in *The Foul and the Fragrant*, by ignoring the history of scents we are 'in danger of misinterpreting [our] dreams and desires. . . . The history of the mignonette, lily and rose is just as informative as the history of coal'.

Chapter Two

Making Scents

Perfumes are created from a harvest of blossom, fruits, spices, resins and woods. The pastoral idyll that once saw farmers stoking up portable stills in fields of lavender has long been replaced by more efficient factory production, but the poetry of perfume lingers. Roses and jasmine are still plucked by hand at dawn in the fields around Grasse, and in tropical locations around the world, pickers with baskets slung round their necks go out into fields redolent with cinnamon, cloves or ylang-ylang to gather the crop. The animals hunted for secretions that give a sexual tang to perfume are increasingly left to live in peace, their allure now mostly reproduced synthetically. And it is synthetics, unromantic though they may be, which have transformed perfume in this century and opened up whole new olfactory landscapes to the art of the perfumer.

Plant Ingredients

To stand at dawn in May in a rose field near Grasse is to witness the last vestige of the old rural life of Europe. The cool, crystalline breath of roses hangs in the air. The fields are full of gypsies and itinerant workers from Italy, Portugal, Algeria and Tunisia, many of them women dressed in sprigged cotton dresses and aprons, each with a sack tied round her waist, some with babies at their knees. They work their way up and down the dew-laden bushes, plucking only the fully opened blossoms, and tossing them into the sacks. Later in the summer, when school's over, the children will join them for the jasmine harvest. It's like a scene from Thomas Hardy's *Tess of the d'Urbervilles*, but one you can no longer find anywhere in England, where a lone farmer in his tractor has replaced this kind of rural community.

In this century, perfume has become big business, but it still has its roots in the land. The fields of flowers around Grasse are nearly gone, replaced by the concrete of roads and real estate. But in other parts of the world, the fragrant crop of plants that is still the bedrock of perfumery is harvested in a similar, labour-intensive way. It's the high cost of labour and land in the south of France that has ousted the fields of flowers from what was once the perfume capital of the world. Jasmine from Grasse costs 15 times as much as jasmine from Egypt. It

Rose de mai or May rose was once grown in great profusion around Grasse, in the south of France. A few precious fields still remain, producing rose absolute for the world's finest fragrance.

makes economic sense, therefore, to use Egyptian or Indian jasmine in a fragrance. Often, perfumers will blend jasmine from different sources, adding just a dash of jasmine de Grasse if the budget allows.

Fragrances are like their aromatic counterparts, wine. The soil, micro-climate and the variety of each flower influences its scent enormously. If you sat down with four samples of jasmine absolute from Grasse, Italy, India and Egypt and sniffed each one, you would instantly smell the difference. The Indian jasmine smells quite savage and raw. It has more indole in it than the others, an element that adds an animal note. The Egyptian jasmine is headier, a little hysterical and peppery. 'It's because the sun burns it there,' a perfume-broker once explained to me. The Italian jasmine is fruity. Not that they don't all smell glorious – until you test the jasmine from Grasse. Like a good perfume composed by a perfumer, the secret of this jasmine is that it is beautifully balanced. It smells rounded, complete, no single note dominates, nothing jars. It is light, cool, elegant. At the same time it is a deliriously narcotic smell.

Best-selling classic fragrances like Chanel No 5, Joy by Patou and Femme by Rochas were formulated decades ago using jasmine or rose from Grasse when the perfume-crop industries in other countries were in their infancy. Because the exact bouquet of rose de mai and jasmine de Grasse cannot be reproduced anywhere else, the makers of these fragrances are obliged to continue buying it. Perfumers often point out that customers are quick to detect that 'something is wrong' with a favourite fragrance. It's not worth saving money at the risk of alienating these customers.

The damask rose (*Rosa damascena*) is grown in Turkey, *above*, as well as Bulgaria and other countries. The rose-pickers are out in the fields at dawn and must pluck thousands of blooms in a few hours, before the essential oil retreats deeper within the plant towards noon. An old Bulgarian proverb says, 'The best attar comes from wet skirts.'

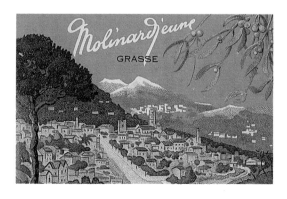

Grasse, once the perfume capital of the world, is still important for the processing of many natural fragrance ingredients.

Chanel No 5 contains a huge 10 per cent of jasmine de Grasse which could be jeopardized by small fluctuations in the jasmine production of the area. Consequently, Chanel has set up a partnership with one of the biggest growers in the Grasse area, the Mul family. The Muls own the fields, but Chanel contracts to buy the majority of the rose and jasmine harvest, and together they have built a small processing plant in the fields.

Although the cultivation of perfumed plants has fallen dramatically in the Grasse area, many of the world's essential oils come here to be brokered on the scent stock market. Most of the brokers are based here, though a few are in Paris. Some ingredients, such as oakmoss, are still sent to Grasse for processing, and a few perfume houses, like Fragonard and Molinard, still produce some perfumes using old semi-artisanal methods in Grasse. But the days when the very water running in the gutters smelt of flower essences, as it still did as recently as the 1960s, are now gone forever.

Sicilian lemon is often used in colognes and fresh fragrances. Here some of it is still hand-pressed, whereas in California the process is highly mechanized.

Right: The roots of vetiver, a grass grown in India, Réunion (right), Java and the West Indies, are distilled for perfume. Indians weave it into sunscreens and mats which are dampened in the morning. As they dry, the cooling vetiver fragrance is wafted through the house.

THE GLOBAL HARVEST

Walk into the chilled storehouse of a perfume-broker and you can smell the whole planet in one place. The labels on the bulging bales and packages that surround you are inescapably exotic: Lavender from Bulgaria; Ginger from The Indies; Coriander from Russia; Geranium from China; Attar of Roses from Turkey; Patchouli from Indonesia; Rosewood from Brazil; Ylang-ylang from the Comoros; Tuberose from India; Jasmine from Morocco. Fragrance is a truly international business that stretches to every continent of the globe.

Several raw ingredients cost as much as or several times their weight in gold, like orris from iris roots, natural musk, jasmine and tuberose. This is because many yield only tiny amounts of essential oil, and the effort involved to extract them is huge: for example, 1 ton of jasmine flowers yields just 1 kg (2 lb) of absolute. As 8,000 blossoms weigh 1 kg (2 lb), it takes 8,000,000 jasmine flowers to make just 1 kg (2 lb) of absolute.

ESSENTIAL OILS

The fragrant essences extracted from a plant are known as its essential oils, also used in aromatherapy. About 2,000 essential oils are known, of which 600–700 are commonly used in perfumery. They are the volatile substances (i.e. they evaporate readily) mainly encapsulated in the cellular glands on the surface of leaves and blossoms, but also in cells deep within other parts of the plant. Unlike other oils, they are not very greasy, and mostly evaporate with hardly a stain.

The quantity and quality of oil a plant releases changes throughout the day, so many fragrance crops have to picked at a specific time. Roses, for example, are picked drenched with dew in the early morning. 'The best attar comes from wet skirts,' says an old Bulgarian proverb. The flowers' oil content decreases by up to 40 per cent by mid-morning.

When we hear the word 'fragrance' we think of a flower, but the essential oils come from many different parts: roots, leaves, bark, stems, seeds, fruits and resins as well as blossoms. The orange tree, for example, yields three essential oils: neroli from the flowers, bitter orange from the fruit peel, and petitgrain or bigarade from the leaves, all smelling completely different. The bitter orange or Seville orange is the most commonly used for perfumery.

Oils from plants

Leaves	*myrtle, patchouli, thyme*
Flowers	*jasmine, mimosa, rose, tuberose, ylang-ylang*
Seed	*almond, carrot, celery, parsley, tonka bean*
Fruit	*nutmeg, pepper, vanilla*
Peel	*bergamot, grapefruit, lemon, lime, orange*
Needles	*Douglas fir, pine*
Wood	*cedar, pine, rosewood, sandalwood*
Bark	*cinnamon, cascarilla*
Roots	*vetiver, orris (from iris tubers)*
Lichen	*oakmoss*
Grass	*citronella, lemongrass, palma rosa*
Tree resins	*frankincense, labdanum, myrrh, opopanax*
Entire plant	*lavender, peppermint, basil*

Jasmine is harvested in many countries, including India. The Indian name for it is 'moonlight of the grove', because it opens by night and closes its blooms during the day.

EXTRACTION

The methods used to extract fragrant oils today are based on the ancient principles of maceration, expression and steam distillation. An 'absolute' is an extract obtained by extraction with volatile solvents or by enfleurage. It is considered the purest perfume material, retaining most of the plant's aromatic constituents. An 'essential oil' is extracted by expression or distillation. The old term 'attar' or 'otto', as in attar of roses, also describes an essential oil obtained by distillation. The word 'attar' comes from the ancient Persian *atr jul* – fat of a flower.

Enfleurage and maceration

Enfleurage goes back thousands of years to the ancient Egyptians. It works on the principle that fats absorb smells in just the same way that butter does in the fridge.

A mixture of beef suet and lard, preserved with benzoin and deodorized with a little rose absolute, is smeared on to a glass plate in a wooden frame called a chassis. The flowers are placed on the fat and left to release their oils, in the case of jasmine for 24 hours and tuberose for 48, then replaced until the fat is saturated. This fragrant pommade is mechanically mixed with alcohol for up to a week, while being chilled down

Enfleurage (*above and left*) is a costly, labour-intensive process that yields the highest quality absolutes because it does not involve heat, which always alters a fragrance. It is used for delicate flowers that don't stand up well to the high heat involved in distillation, and only works for flowers that continue to release essential oils once they are picked – like jasmine and tuberose. Flower heads are placed one by one on a glass plate smeared with fat in a wooden chassis (*left*). These are stacked and left for a day or two for the flowers to release their oils. The frames are tipped up to release the spent flowers, and fresh flower heads are applied until the fat is saturated with the oil, a process that can take up to a month.

to –20°C (–68°F) until every molecule of the flowers' essential oil in the fat is dissolved out into the alcohol. (Fat does not dissolve in alcohol.) At this point, the mixture is a highly scented slurry. It is chilled further and filtered several times to remove all the fat.

The alcohol is then evaporated, leaving the pure absolute. This labour-intensive method of extraction is little used today. Very fine fragrances like those by Guerlain and Chanel sometimes contain a small amount of this liquid jewel. Even at concentrations as low as 1 part in 10,000, jasmine extracted in this way adds an inimitable transparency to a fragrance.

Maceration is similar to enfleurage. It is used for animal ingredients, and occasionally tonka beans, vanilla and iris. The raw material is sifted into vats of oil or alcohol and steeped for long periods, sometimes years, until all its odorous parts dissolve. In some cases, the oil is heated to encourage the process. The hot process yields an infusion; cold maceration yields a tincture. In India, you can still find a fragrance dating back thousands of years, Chameli Ka Tel, which is made by macerating jasmine flowers in sesame oil.

Expression

Expression is a simple technique where the rinds of citrus fruits are cold-pressed to extract their essential oils using rollers or sponges. The fact that no heat is involved means that the resulting oils smell very close to the living plant.

Distillation

This is the main method used for extracting essential oils. It has been verified only recently that distillation was known in ancient times and stills have been found at the ancient cities of Nineveh on the Tigris and Mohenjo Daro and Taxila on the Indus, dating back 5,000 years. The process was lost to the West but preserved and continually improved by the Arabs. Avicenna, the great Arab philosopher and scientist, is usually credited with inventing the alembic or still, but older

Ylang-ylang is distilled in simple processing plants among the fields in the French colony of Réunion. Here, a worker is tipping the flowers into an alembic for steam distillation.

Arab texts in fact show that the process of distillation was perfected by the ninth century AD.

The process is based on the principle that when plants are boiled with water, the essential oils, which are volatile (the reason we so readily smell them), will vaporize and rise up with the steam. The alembic (from the Arab *al inbik*, meaning a still) is a cauldron with a lid which has a pipe for collecting the rising vapour. The pipe then leads downward into a collecting vessel. Improvements by the Arabs resulted in the coiled serpentine pipe whose large surface area allows more of the oil and steam to condense back into liquids.

Before distillation, roots and herbs are crushed and woods grated to encourage them to release their locked-in essential oils. Flowers and leaves, where the oils are close to the surface,

Extraction with volatile solvents

This method is used for delicate flowers whose odours are damaged by the high heat needed to boil water. The oils are extracted using petrochemical solvents which have a lower boiling point than water, with a method similar to distillation.

need no treatment. The plants are then placed in the alembic. At one time, this would have contained copious quantities of water and the mixture would have been boiled. Today, the plants are layered on to grilles and superheated steam is passed through them. This more intense heat allows aromatic elements with very high boiling points to be released.

The mixture of steam and essential oils rises into a pipe known as a swan's neck and down into the coiled cooling pipe, the serpentine, where the steam and oils condense back into liquid. In old distilleries the copper coils of the serpentine were clearly visible, but today they are hidden inside another vat which contains a constant flow of cool water to encourage condensation.

The mixture of essential oils and water is collected at the bottom in a narrow container called a Florentine vase. Because essential oils are generally lighter than water, they rise to the top of the vat, where they are tapped off. The water is collected from a tap at the bottom and recycled. In some cases, as with rosewater and orange-flower water, the distilled water retaining traces of essential oil is sold separately as a by-product.

Opposite: For extraction with volatile solvents, the roses are shovelled on to grilles and steeped with hot solvents until the oils and waxes are dissolved out. At this point, the mixture is siphoned off and, when the extractor is opened, the spent roses remain, forming a surreal 'wedding cake'.

Below: Concrète of rose de mai is deep red and semi-solid since it still contains the waxes and pigments of the flower.

This is the process used today to extract essential oils of rose de mai and jasmine and many others. Sacks of roses gathered by the pickers are emptied into an extractor which is divided into layers by plates of perforated metal so that the weight of the flowers doesn't crush and damage those underneath. The solvent is piped in and the mixture is gently heated. The solvent dissolves the essential oils, vegetable waxes and rose pigment. Leaving the spent roses behind, this mixture is then piped into an alembic where it is brought to the boil, like an amber-tinted stew, evaporating the solvent. What is left are all the plant extracts, which, because of the waxes, form a solid substance called a 'concrète', as in *concrète de rose*. Concrètes are used in products like soaps, and in solid perfumes, which are rare nowadays.

For use in perfumes, the waxes and most of the pigment must be removed, leaving pure essential oil. To get this, the concrète is greatly chilled and stirred mechanically with alcohol, forming, in the case of roses, a deep-pink slush, which is then filtered to remove the suspended waxes and most of the pigment. The alcohol-essential oil mixture is then gently heated in an alembic so that the alcohol evaporates, leaving a floral absolute. The search for solvents with even lower boiling points which can be used for even more delicate flowers is an on-going process.

Pickers carry their baskets of Indian jasmine flowers from the fields to be weighed. Picking stops by mid-morning when the flowers begin to close, and the flower heads must then be processed on the spot before their freshness fades.

PLANT PORTRAITS

Flowers

Many flower fragrances are used in perfumery, although synthetics are increasingly used in their place. A number of flower ingredients are still extracted from nature, however, and here we look at some of the most famous, together with one (violet) which is no longer distilled but is now composed from a mixture of synthetics and other flowers.

Jasmine

In Grasse, jasmine is known simply as *la fleur* ('the flower'). In India it is called 'moonlight of the grove' because the flowers open at night to release their heady fragrance and close by day. In the Grasse area, the pickers are out before dawn when the odour is at its most intense, each with a wicker basket in which to put the blossoms. Jasmine can't be collected in the usual sack because the flowers bruise easily, and this causes them to release more indole, unbalancing the flower's natural bouquet.

Getting jasmine essential oil from a field of blooms is like getting blood from a stone. Eight thousand flowers yield only 1 g ($\frac{1}{25}$ oz) of absolute. The pickers fill their baskets and take the flowers to be weighed immediately. Each is paid in cash according to how much she has collected. A champion jasmine-picker will gather around 2 kg ($4\frac{1}{2}$ lb) of flowers a day.

Jasmine originates from India and the Arabian Gulf where more than a hundred scented types are known. It was brought to Provence in about 1560. Nowadays, it is cultivated in Morocco, using modern production methods, India, Egypt, Italy and Turkey. *Jasminum grandiflorum* is the species most grown for perfume.

Jasmine is a jewel among perfumery flowers, the most widely used of all the white flowers. It, or its synthetic counterparts, are found in 83 per cent of all women's fragrances and about 33 per cent of all men's fragrances. Its mysterious attraction lies in the way the rich flux of its perfume is undercut with a carnal taint of flesh, due to its high percentage of indole. By itself, indole smells like a wet fur coat. In minute dosage, like many perfume constituents, it takes on a different character, which marries with the human body scent. Nowadays, due to the prohibitive expense of producing jasmine, its principal odour-chemical, cis-jasmone, is often substituted, with a certain amount of indole.

Rose

Some time between 4000 and 2000 BC, a lovelorn Sumerian sent the object of his affections a vase of perfume together with a tablet inscribed with this message: 'This little vase contains 100 rose petals from my garden, but each petal expresses a thought of love for you.' This may be 6,000-year-old schmaltz, but it shows that the connection between roses and romance is as old as civilization.

Rose perfumes were adored by the Romans and the Greeks. Roman myth relates that the goddess Flora stumbled on the body of a beautiful nymph and, with the help of Venus and the Graces, transformed her into the rose. The Persians were probably the first to distil rosewater and they exported hundreds of thousands of bottles a year throughout antiquity and right up to the Middle Ages.

Roses are a very ancient flower. Fossils of wild roses date back as much as 40 million years. Rose oil, or attar of roses, comes chiefly from two species. *Rosa centifolia*, the cabbage rose, and its hybrids are grown in the South of France round Grasse, and also today in North Africa. It is known to the Grasseois as 'rose de mai' or 'rose de Grasse'. It has a lemony top note, a sherbety heart note and a spicy dry-down. The scent is lighter and crisper than that of

Rosa damascena, or damask rose, which is the most widely grown for perfumery. Rose de mai is extracted using solvents.

The damask rose is cultivated in Bulgaria, at the foot of the Balkan Mountains in the largest rose-growing centre in the world, in Turkey, Iran and India. It was the species most used by the early Arab perfumers. The scent is heavier and more velvety than that of rose de mai. It is extracted by distillation. A hectare (2.5 acres) of rose bushes can yield up to 3,000 kg (6,600 lb) of petals.

While rose appears in about three-quarters of all fine fragrances, it is difficult to find a single rose note fragrance. Annick Goutal's Rose Absolute is a blend of six varieties of attar of roses; old English perfumers Floris, who maintain a Victorian tradition of perfumery, offer single flower notes, including Red Rose; and The Perfumer's Workshop, an American company, have a very popular Tea Rose.

The rose is one of the most loved of all flowers used in perfumery.

Rose de mai awaiting processing into absolute at the Roure distillery in Grasse. A champion rose-picker can pick up to 50 kg (110 lb) a day, but this yields only a few drops of rose oil.

Orange blossom is grown in Tunisia, where this bloom is from, as well as other warm countries. It is an indispensable component of eau de Cologne and many other scents.

Neroli

Neroli or orange-flower oil is distilled from the flowers of orange trees, especially, for fine fragrances, the Seville or bitter-orange tree. It is grown in the south of France, Spain, Italy and North Africa. It probably originates from India and is thought to have been brought West in about the ninth century AD, though it may have been grown in the Middle East for thousands of years. One beautiful line in the Old Testament is sometimes presumed to refer to oranges: 'A word fitly spoken is like apples of gold in pictures of silver.' And the golden apple offered to Juno by Jupiter on her wedding day is thought to have been an orange. Arab brides wore orange blossom as a symbol of fecundity, and the Crusaders brought this custom to Christian brides, who still traditionally include orange blossom in their wedding bouquets. In China, orange blossom is used to flavour Orange Pekoe tea.

Orange-flower oil got its name in the seventeenth century from the Italian Princess of Neroli. She began the fashion for using it to scenting gloves, which were named *guanti di Neroli* after her. The oil is extracted by water distillation, and the water used is decanted after removal of the neroli oil and sold as orange-flower water. When

The sweet violet yields only a microscopic amount of oil, so a composed perfume of synthetics and orris root is used for violet scents instead. The leaves, however, are still distilled.

the oil is extracted using volatile solvents or by maceration, first a concrète is produced, then an absolute called orange-flower absolute, which has a different smell from neroli. Both oils are used in perfumery – for example, Claude Montana's Montana and Estée Lauder's Beautiful use orange-flower oil, while neroli is found in many oriental and floriental fragrances.

Neroli oil has an intense, sweet aroma complicated by the sultry faecal note of indole, also found in jasmine.

Violet

One of the most charming scenes round nineteenth-century Grasse must have been the young girls in their bonnets scattered under the olive trees in early springtime gathering baskets of violets to be macerated for perfume. But violets are hardly grown in the region today, although their fragrance is one of the most universally beloved.

Diane Ackerman, in *A Natural History of the Senses*, describes it best: 'violets smell like burnt sugar cubes that have been dipped in lemon and velvet.'

Although Josephine was a great lover of musk, she also wore a violet perfume, and Napoleon planted violets at her grave. Before his exile to St

of a minute.' Soon after smelling them, the odour vanishes, only to return after some minutes. The Victorians made a cult of the violet, which with its shy, haunting scent symbolized the melancholy and wavering nature of love. The French author Michelet equates it with woman herself in *La Femme*: 'Its love-dust flies away in the wind; it must be well protected, held back, above all, fertilized.'

The ancients esteemed it highly as a perfume and a medicine. Pliny recommended a wreath of violets wound through the hair to cure a headache. In recent centuries, an infusion of the leaves was drunk as a cure for cancer, and even today, violet petal syrup can be bought in many pharmacies.

Two varieties of violet are used for perfumery, the Victoria violet and the Parma violet grown especially in northern Italy. The oil of the latter is considered the finest. Violet oil can be extracted by maceration or using volatile solvents. It is extremely expensive because the flower yields only a microscopic amount and is no longer seriously grown for perfumery. Since ionone was synthesized in 1898, violet has been accurately reproduced as a 'composed fragrance', which is the name given to a fragrance that aims to imitate a natural flower using other ingredients. In the case of violet, orris absolute is used together with synthetics like the ionones and extracts from other plant sources.

An essential oil is extracted from the leaves as well, and this is occasionally blended into a violet perfume to give a fresh, crushed leaf fragrance that more accurately reproduces the effect of inhaling the scent of the living plant.

You can smell the violet in Chanel No 19, Givenchy's L'Interdit and Balmain's Jolie Madame, among others.

Helena, he plucked some of these violets and kept them in a locket round his neck, which he wore until his death.

Violets have a peculiarly elusive quality. As Shakespeare put it, they are: 'Forward, not permanent, sweet, not lasting/The perfume and suppliance

Orange flowers are collected in North Africa by shaking the branches and twigs so that the blossoms fall on to sacking spread under the tree.

Lime
2, 4, 5, 6, 7, 8

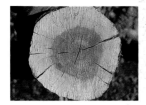

Orris
13, 22

Sandalwood
36, 44, 46, 47

Tuberose
13, 19, 30, 32, 36, 40

Rose
13, 18, 19, 26, 27, 30

Perfume plants come from all over the world. This map shows some of the many diverse plants and where they are found.

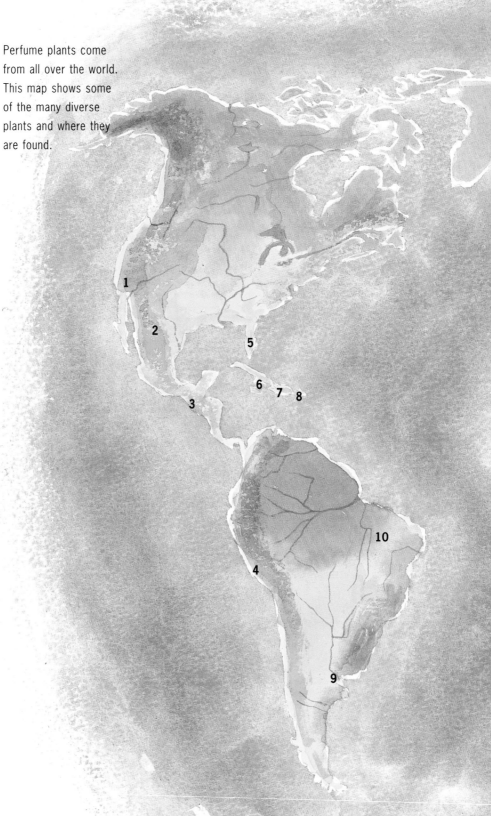

Jasmine
13, 16, 18, 19, 22, 25,
27, 30, 32, 36, 39

Ylang-ylang
32, 33, 41

Vanilla
2, 32, 34, 35, 38,
42, 43

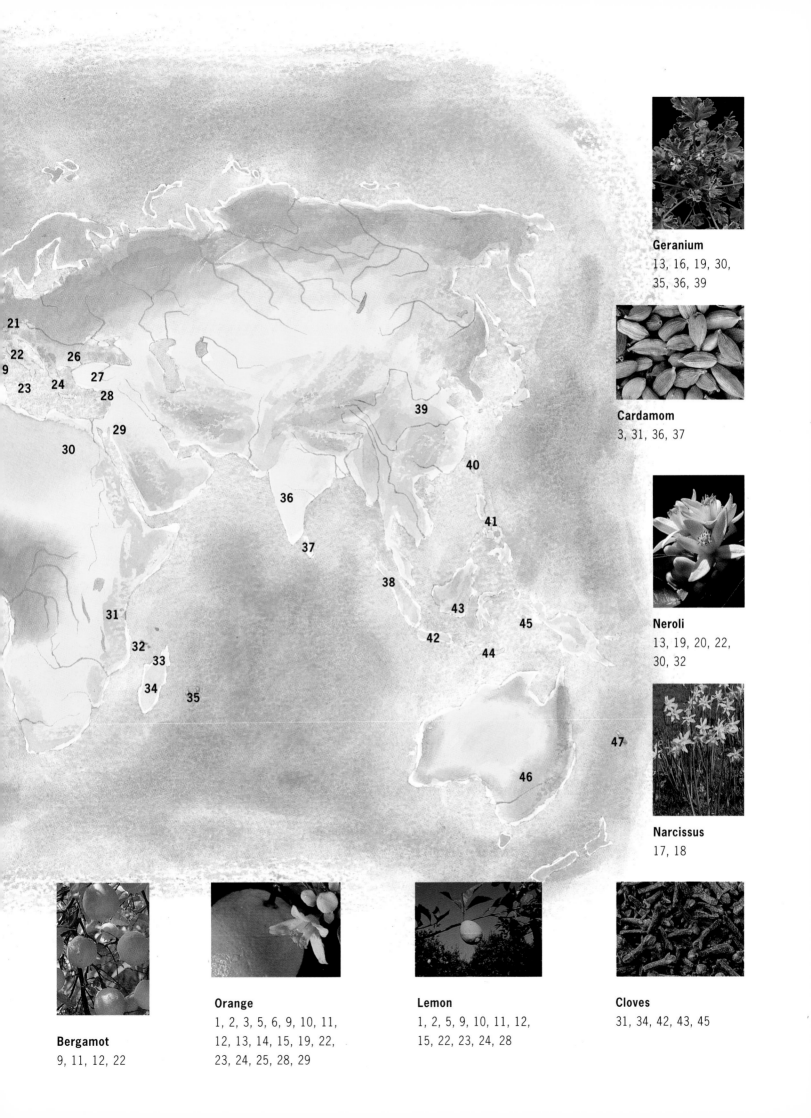

Geranium
13, 16, 19, 30,
35, 36, 39

Cardamom
3, 31, 36, 37

Neroli
13, 19, 20, 22,
30, 32

Narcissus
17, 18

Bergamot
9, 11, 12, 22

Orange
1, 2, 3, 5, 6, 9, 10, 11,
12, 13, 14, 15, 19, 22,
23, 24, 25, 28, 29

Lemon
1, 2, 5, 9, 10, 11, 12,
15, 22, 23, 24, 28

Cloves
31, 34, 42, 43, 45

Ylang-ylang

Ylang-ylang was an ingredient of the famous Macassar hair oil of the nineteenth century and is now widely used for fine fragrance. Its name means 'flower of flowers' in the language of the Moluccan Islanders. The tree grows

Ylang-ylang does not develop its powerfully sweet fragrance until two to three weeks after the buds have opened.

throughout south-east Asia, where it has been valued for its rich, heavy perfume for centuries. Women weave it into garlands and wear it in their hair. The Balinese make it the centrepiece of flower-offerings to their gods.

Once the ylang-ylang flowers have been gathered, they need to be processed quickly in small distilleries set up for the purpose among the trees.

Ylang-ylang is grown for perfumery in the Philippines, Réunion and the Comoro Islands near Madagascar, and Java. The finest oil comes from the Philippines. The *Cananga odorata* tree grows up to 20 m (65 ft) high and produces clusters of golden-yellow flowers which blossom throughout the year. They give off no detectable fragrance until they have been open for two or three weeks, after which they must be gathered quickly. The best flowers are mature, on the point of withering, with a tinge of red in the heart. The flowers are gathered in the early morning by women and children with sacks slung round their necks. They are processed on the spot by steam distillation yielding an oil of cloying, tropical sweetness that has become highly popular in modern perfumery but must be used with discretion. Cananga oil, from a related tree, is substituted in cheaper perfumes, although synthetic ylang-ylang is also used.

Resins

Resins are often said to be the oldest perfume ingredients. Certainly, they were the most valued of ancient times, important in religious ceremonies and as medicines as well as, later, profane perfumes. The incense common to many religions is basically resins. Frankincense and myrrh are still burned in the great Christian cathedrals together with benzoin (or gum benjamin) and rosemary. At Notre Dame in Paris, for example, a special incense burned at Easter contains resins with cinnamon rolled in real gold dust.

Resins are gummy substances that either ooze spontaneously from the barks of some trees or are obtained by cutting into the tree. They are like a tree's equivalent of a scab, secreted to protect them from infection when the bark is damaged. They are also known as gum-resins, balsams and balms. Myrrh, frankincense (sometimes just called incense or olibanum), styrax or storax from the liquidamber tree, labdanum, galbanum, opopanax and balsam of Peru are among the best-known resins. They are long-lasting base notes.

Frankincense

In the great days of the frankincense trade, these amber lumps of resin were as precious as diamonds. Workers at the ancient processing plant in Alexandria were strictly guarded and, according to Pliny the Elder, forced to take off all their clothes before leaving, to deter smuggling.

In Arabia today, frankincense is still used in all the ancient ways, as part of religious ritual, as a medicine and as a purifying perfume. The Bedouin stand above small censers filled with smouldering frankincense wood and allow the fragrant smoke to permeate

The great wealth of southern Arabia in ancient times was built on the resin got by chipping away the bark of these small, wizened trees. Frankincense is still used as incense in the Catholic church and as a medicine in the Arabian peninsula. It is used in about 13 per cent of modern perfumes, especially those belonging to the oriental family.

their robes. Arabs of the Gulf use the ground-up powder of the resin as a medicine for stomach upsets, and chew another type to clean the teeth and gums and clear the head.

Frankincense comes from *Boswellia sacra*, a small, shrubby, wizened tree native to the desert regions of the Arabian peninsula and the horn of Africa. The bark is chipped away until it sweats milky white tears that gradually solidify into runnels of golden resin on exposure to air. The trees are tapped all year round, but it is highly labour-intensive work.

Arabia Felix, centre of the great perfume trade of Biblical times, still produces the best frankincense and myrrh, although cheaper incense from India and Somalia is now the main source. At the height of trade, when frankincense travelled by caravan through the desert along the Incense Route up to Petra in what is now Jordan, south Arabia exported more than 3,000 tons a year to Rome and Greece alone. It was an incredibly lucrative trade which the Arabs operated as a cartel, like an ancient version of OPEC. Now the Arab countries export only a few tons a year.

Myrrh

In the time of the ancients, myrrh cost three times as much as frankincense, but frankincense was in five times greater demand. Myrrh was used in the embalming of Egyptian mummies; it is highly antiseptic and an excellent preservative. The first recorded mention of this venerable perfume ingredient is on the fifteenth-century BC tomb of Queen Hatshepsut. It was also the chief ingredient in the sacred anointing oil of the Jews. Some sources contend that the myrrh of ancient times was actually opopanax, sometimes called sweet myrrh, produced from a related tree. The Romans and Greeks called it 'stacte'.

The thorny, scrubby myrrh tree *Commiphora myrrha* grows in the same regions as the frankincense tree. Herodotus the Greek wrote of Arabia and its resins in 450 BC: 'The whole country is scented with them and exhales an odour marvellously sweet.' Myrrh is used in a small percentage of modern perfumes like Amouage, Roma by Laura Biagiotti, Opium by Yves Saint Laurent, and Salvador Dali.

Labdanum

Often called 'amber' by perfumers, this oily resin is very important to modern perfumery because its smell somewhat resembles ambergris, from whales, which is becoming increasingly unobtainable. It comes from shrubs of the Cistus genus, commonly called the rock rose, native to the Mediterranean and the Middle East. The resin oozes out from the stems and forms drops on the undersides of the leaves. Ambrein, one of its constituents, is the main ingredient in synthetic ambers.

Labdanum probably wasn't known to the earliest Egyptians,

Labdanum is used in oriental fragrances as a substitute for ambergris, now in short supply.

but Herodotus listed it as a main perfumery ingredient in the fifth century BC, imported by caravan from Arabia. The Arabs combed it off the beards of goats that had been sent to browse among the bushes. Dioscorides later described it being collected by stroking a leather thong over the leaves, a method which is still used in Cyprus. It was one of the essential ingredients in the original chypre ('Cyprus') perfume of ancient times.

Woods

Sandalwood

In India, agarbatti or incense sticks daubed with sandalwood paste have been used for thousands of years for religious purification and fumigation. Temples were often built with sandalwood walls as the wood is impervious to white ants, and Hindus still use powdered sandalwood (*chandana*) made into a paste to mark their foreheads with a tikka for men or a bindi for women. In ninth-century Ceylon, it was used to embalm the royal corpses.

Sandalwood has a distinctly complex character, being at times cool and cerebral, and at others intensely aphrodisiac. The Hindus were also well aware of its erotic overtones, and Indian courtesans rubbed their breasts with sandalwood paste mixed with musk to increase their allure. It contains a steroid molecule similar to testosterone, the hormone that drives the libido in both men and women.

The essential oil comes from the white sandalwood tree, which grows wild in the forests of southern India – 85 per cent of the sandalwood grown for perfume comes from the province of Mysore alone.

Sandalwood has exotic feeding habits. It is a hemiparasite, using octopus-like suckers to drink nutrients from the roots of neighbouring trees and plants. Eventually, vampire-like, it bleeds its hosts – usually bamboo and guava – to death. The oil is found in the heartwood and roots, and mature trees must be felled to obtain it. The best oil comes from trees that are 30–60 years old. Harvesting is strictly controlled by the Indian government. Such a large quantity of sandalwood is used in Guerlain's Samsara that the company bought its own plantations in India to ensure a steady supply. Sandalwood is a superb fixative, sometimes lingering for days.

Agarwood

Although you may never smell this wood – also called aloeswood or lignum aloes – you should know about it; it is one of the most extraordinary ingredients in perfumery. The 'aloes'

Sandalwood being chipped in preparation for distillation.

referred to in the Bible and other ancient texts was probably this wood, the scent of which has been compared to a blend of sandalwood and ambergris. Certainly 'aloes' was not the modern aloe vera used in cosmetics.

The Arabs call it oud and I first smelt it when I lived in Abu Dhabi. Its austere, resinous yet strangely sensual fragrance accompanied the Arabs everywhere, and in the desert I watched Bedouins light a charcoal fire on a small incense-burner, scatter tiny slivers of oud on top and stand over it, waving their long robes in the odorous smoke so that it would form an ambrosial nimbus of scent around their bodies.

It is by far the most expensive ingredient in perfumery. You can buy it in the Arab souks, but it is becoming increasingly rare, and fakes are often passed off. I finally obtained some of the extracted oil, known as agar attar or churrah, in Lucknow in India, renowned for its perfumes.

Agarwood oil is formed when a fungus attacks the tree *Aquilaria agallocha*, which grows in north-east India, Malaysia and parts of China. The fungus, which only affects mature trees about 50 years old, causes the heartwood to darken and develop an oleoresin or oily resin not found in healthy trees. The normal wood is light, but the oil-charged wood is so heavy it sinks in water and the Chinese call it *ch'en hsiang* or 'sinking fragrance'.

After long distillation, the oleoresin yields an essential oil. The Japanese, great connoisseurs of incense, also prize it above all others, calling it *jinko*. Today Japanese industrialists and Arab sheikhs pay kings' ransoms for sections of the wood. The perfume is so sought after that agarwood trees have been reduced almost to extinction.

Fruits, leaves and roots

Vanilla

Vanilla was discovered in 1520 by
Hernando Cortés in Mexico, where
the Aztecs used it to flavour their
chocolate drinks, and is now grown
commercially in the West Indies,
Réunion, Tahiti and Madagascar. It
is a product of the vanilla orchid
vine which winds itself round trees
and feeds on air: it is an epiphytic
plant. The fruit pods are picked,
dipped in warm water, then packed
in barrels lined in wool to sweat for
a day. This is followed by a week-
long exposure to the sun before
they are spread onto trays in the
drying sheds. Here, during a six-
month fermentation and drying
process, white crystals containing
the essential oil form a frost on the
surface of the pods. The caressing,
fondant aroma of vanilla is present

Vanilla pods exposed to
dry in the sun.

Dried patchouli leaves,
a key element of chypre
fragrances.

in the vast majority of all fine
fragrances today, although vanillin, the
principal odiferous chemical in the
plant, made synthetically, is now often
substituted.

Patchouli

With its sour odour of raw, damp
jungle undergrowth, patchouli is a
unique perfume ingredient used
especially in fougère and chypre
fragrances and about half of all
men's fragrances. It is the strongest
aroma in the plant kingdom, and
one of the longest-lasting base
notes. Hippies wore patchouli in
the 1960s and '70s and burned it
as incense because its odour masks
the smell of marijuana.

The attar is extracted from the
leaves of the patchouli plant,
Pogostemon patchouli, which
reaches about 1 m (3 ft) in height
and is grown in India, Indonesia,

Sri Lanka, the Seychelles and along the Malaysian coast. It is harvested by simply being cut down like silage and baled. The bales both dry and ferment during shipping to Europe for extraction by steam distillation. A less pure oil is obtained by distillation in the fields and redistilled on arrival in Europe.

Patchouli began to be used in Europe in about 1826 as a result of the mania for Indian shawls. These paisley shawls were faked by the Scots and French, who were frustrated in their early attempts because the much more valuable Indian originals could be identified through a peculiar odour. Eventually, they realized it was due to patchouli and imported the oil to perfume their imitations. Patchouli is still used in India to scent the laundry and discourage insects.

Orris

Orris is the dried rhizomes or bulbs of the iris plant, and is one of the most important perfumery materials. The soft, powdery scent is similar to violet and it is often mixed with synthetic ionone to make violet perfumes. However, it is an even finer scent, deep, woody, soft and warm, harmonizing closely with some people's body-scent. For this reason, it is considered aphrodisiac. It can be smelt clearly in Chanel's No 19. It is prohibitively expensive: true orris concrète costs about US$15,000 for 1 kg (2 lb), and the rarely available oil ten times as much.

The rhizomes are stored, aged and dried on wooden shelves in a kind of iris sauna known as a 'warm room' for two years, then powdered and steam-distilled, unusually, for between three

Orris root is dried for two years to acquire its characteristic powdery fragrance. It is used to give a violet scent to perfumes.

The distillation process yields a very viscous concrète known as orris butter.

and six months continually. The continuous redistillation is necessary because of the tiny quantity of oil in the powdered root. The resulting gooey yellow concrète is called orris butter.

Several varieties are used for perfumery, especially *Iris pallida*, which yields the best oil, and the Florentine iris, grown around Florence in Italy. Orris is also cultivated in France, Morocco and India.

Orris root has been prized as a perfume since the time of the ancient Greeks because of its violet scent. Macedonia and Corinth were renowned for their iris unguents made by powdering the root. From the Middle Ages, it was the base of many European powdered perfumes hung in sachets from the body, dusted into the hair or slipped into the linen closet, and it was made into beads for rosaries. The iris, regarded as a symbol of kingship since ancient times, gets its name from the Greek goddess of the rainbow.

Animal Ingredients

If you unstoppered a bottle of raw castoreum tincture extracted from beavers, a foul, persistent miasma would stun your nostrils into horrified submission. Diluted at a strength of just one part per thousand in a floral blend, however, it would give a glorious effect. The scent would develop the richness and warmth that only an animal note can give. As perfumer Arthur Burnham puts it, 'a rose without civet is like a steak without salt'. Animal notes are sexy and very close chemically to our own sexual aromas. Melting and merging with the skin's own musky scent, they add something mysterious and fascinating to the pastoral simplicity of flowers. As such, they are an essential part of many commercial fragrances.

Animal extracts are always used in minute concentrations because of their overpowering odour. The raw ingredient is steeped in alcohol until the odorous components are dissolved, then it is filtered to form a tincture as in 'tincture of musk'. Sometimes at a processing factory you will see a strange table rocking continuously from side to side, loaded with pear-shaped flasks full of dark liquid. These are tinctures, which are shaken in this way for six months or so until all the fragrant part is dissolved in the alcohol. Nowadays, the vast majority of animal notes are reproduced synthetically due to their prohibitive cost and the increasing difficulty of ensuring a steady supply of the real thing.

A 1772 French engraving shows some of the animals that yield perfume secretions. On the sea floats a lump of ambergris, while in the foreground a civet, then known as a zibeth, stands forlornly in his cage, and an oriental gentleman stabs an unfortunate musk deer. The man with the comb is collecting labdanum from the goat's beard.

Ambergris

'Ambergris, n.s. [from *amber* and *gris* or *grey*,]; that is, grey amber. A fragrant drug that melts almost like wax, commonly of a greyish or ash colour, used both as a perfume and a cordial. It is found on the sea coasts of several warm countries, and on the Western coasts of Ireland. Some imagine it to be the excrement of a bird, which, being melted by the heat of the sun, and washed off the shore by the waves, is swallowed by whales, who return it back in the condition we find it. Others conclude it to be the excrement of a cetaceous fish, because sometimes found in the intestines of such animals. . . . Others take it for a kind of wax or gum, which distils from trees, and drops into the sea, where it congeals. Many of the orientals imagine it springs out of the sea, as naphtha does out of some fountains. Others suppose it a sea mushroom, torn up from the bottom by the violence of tempests. . . . Others maintain, that ambergris is made from the honey-combs, which fall into the sea from the rocks, where the bees had formed their nests. . . . Some affirm it to be a true animal concrete, formed in balls in the body of the male spermacity whale, and lodged in a large oval bag over the testicles.' Thus Dr Johnson struggled to define and describe the origins of what is certainly the most mysterious, and was once considered the noblest, substance in perfumery in his famous *Dictionary* of 1755.

Dr Johnson wasn't far off in one of his speculations. Ambergris does indeed come from the belly of a sperm whale, but is a kind of whale vomit rather than excrement.

Even today, no one quite knows why whales produce it. It is thought to be a pathological secretion from the animal's gut, caused by the rough beaks of the squid that form its main diet irritating the lining of the stomach. The weathering of months or years at sea improves the smell. At first, it has a penetrating, pungent odour, but time matures it to a velvety, sleek aroma, suavely musky with a flavour of clean, warm, suntanned skin. The finest is white ambergris, which has spent a long time floating in the sea and is rarely more than a few grammes or ounces in weight. The largest single piece of ambergris ever found weighed 152 kg (336 lb) and came on to the London market in 1913.

Ambergris was unknown to the ancients until the time of Alexander the Great, when one of his admirals collected it up

The sperm whale forms ambergris around the sharp, irritating beaks of squid that lodge in its gut. Ambergris is basically a special kind of whale vomit.

Lumps of ambergris are still collected from beaches where they wash up, but today synthetic substitutes are mostly used in place of real ambergris.

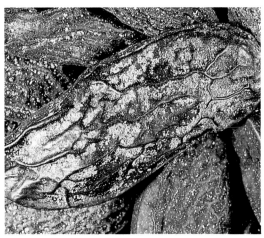

and down the coast of the Gulf of Oman and India in 325 BC. It was one of the important exports of Mahgreb, or Morocco, its cost on a par with gold and black slaves. When they find it today, Moroccans roll it into little balls and let it dissolve in their tea as an aphrodisiac.

In the Middle Ages, ambergris was used like a spice in cooking, and centuries later Casanova praised the invigorating powers of chocolate mousse flavoured with it. The scent, which is considered highly aphrodisiac in the West also, had a prodigious reputation in the eighteenth century. According to Nicolas Lemery's *Dictionary of Drugs* of 1760, 'It fortified the brain, excited joy, generated semen, and helped to counter snake poison.' Its odour lasts for many years, even centuries as a solid perfume. There is a room at Hampton Court in England which still smells faintly of ambergris. It was used for perfuming gloves; Queen Elizabeth I always had her gloves scented with 'amber'.

In the nineteenth and twentieth centuries, ambergris was collected from the sperm whale by whalers. It alone could fetch as much money as the carcass of the whole whale. Nowadays, it has been largely replaced by synthetics and labdanum, though it is still supplied by whalers to some perfume companies, commanding prices around US $7,000 for 1 kg (2 lb).

Jean Gattefossé, the inventor of modern aromatherapy, proposed a fascinating theory about ambergris: Pliny described the ancient Romans as using a pulverized mollusc, *Elodone moschata*, in perfumery. As this cuttlefish is part of the whale's diet, the actual perfume may come from the shellfish.

Castoreum

Not to be confused with castor oil from the castor oil bush, castoreum is a creamy substance packed into egg-shaped sacs in the genital region of beavers of both sexes, used by them to waterproof and scent their coats. It has a foetid odour when undiluted, but as a tincture, it takes on a sultry, leathery, smoky note, much valued in men's perfumery especially. Among women's perfumes, it is used in oriental fragrances. It has been known since the time of Hippocrates, for whom it was a medicine for gynaecological disorders.

The beaver is seen here using its castoreum for the purpose for which it was intended – water-proofing and scenting its coat.

Later, in the Hellenistic period, it garnered a great reputation as an aphrodisiac. Pomet, in his *History of Drugs* (1694), is intriguing about the fakes: 'The dearness of castor and the avarice of wicked persons have induced people to counterfeit it, which they do by mixing the powder of true castor with gums that there is no necessity of naming and putting them in skins, which have contained the testicles of lambs and goats; then they hang them in the chimney and pass them off as true castor.' In fact, in former centuries, it was thought that these scent sacs *were* the beaver's testicles and naturalists wrote how hunted beavers would pause to gnaw off their own testicles frantically and leave them in their path as they knew very well that these were what the hunters really wanted.

Castoreum is a by-product of the fur trade. Beavers are still trapped in significant numbers – for example, in 1984 500,000 beavers were trapped in the USA and Canada, and the trapping of beavers is beginning again in Siberia. However, the synthetic castoreums now available are just as good as the real thing if blended well.

Civet

This is an excretion from the anal glands of the Ethiopian civet cat of both sexes. The wild civet cats are captured and kept in narrow cages by Ethiopian housewives who regularly prod the cats with sticks, as they secrete more civet when angry. The buttery, viscous liquid, which smells appallingly excremental in the raw, is often adulterated with human baby faeces to make it go further (the quality can be determined by weight; pure civet is heavier). It is removed from the animal with a spatula dipped in Vaseline. The cats' hind legs are first tied to the top of the cage and the abdomen pressed to open the glands. This painful process is repeated every ten days or so. Each animal produces about 25–30 g (1–1¼ oz) of civet monthly. The animals are eventually released.

Civet extract hardens and darkens on contact with the air. It is packed into zebu horns, sealed with leather and exported. The treated, diluted scent is similar to musk but more piercing with a smoky, sweaty aroma. The ancients were probably confusing the civet cat with the panther when they described the latter as the 'perfumed panther'. The word for 'panther' and 'courtesan' in ancient Greece was the same.

From the seventeenth century, civet was widely used to flavour pipe tobacco and tobacco-sellers plied their trade by the sign of 'Ye Olde Civette'. At that period, the Dutch merchants kept civets or zibeths at their houses in Amsterdam. It is still used in about 10 per cent of modern perfumes. There are many artifical substitutes now available.

Musk

Musk is secreted by a penile sheath gland of the musk deer, an animal about the size of a goat found near the snowline in the Himalayas and Central Asia. It is produced only when the animals are in rut, suggesting that it performs a sexual role, probably as a scent for marking territory. The musk pod can be extracted without killing the animals, but in practice they are nearly always killed first, and as it is hard to tell females and males apart, many females are uselessly slaughtered.

Musk deer are currently in danger of extinction. The Chinese, however, are experimenting with musk-farms to produce the substance commercially. The international trade in musk is estimated at about 320 kg (700 lb) a year, divided equally between perfumery and oriental medicine. France annually imports about 50 kg (120 lb) of musk but re-exports a third to other European countries and the USA. It has been known to cost as much as US$60,000 for 1 kg (2 lb). In spite of strict controls, the black market is flourishing – a Tibetan who sells two musk pods can live on the proceeds for a year or more.

The gingerbread-like musk grains are found inside a pod-like pouch. The pods are scooped out like scallops from the deer's abdomen. One musk-pod contains about 15–20 g ($\frac{1}{2}$–$\frac{3}{4}$ oz) of musk. They are worth many times their weight in gold and are often adulterated by injecting a mixture of blood, dung and ammonia into the pouch. The odour is intense, faecal, oily and clinging. To some people it is unbearable, others find it irresistibly erogenous. It long held the reputation of giving women 'the vapours', and was considered such a powerful narcotic

Above: Civet is extracted from glands round the anus of the Ethiopian civet cat. The cats use it as a sexual attractant and territory-marker.

Left: The thick, buttery oil is scraped from the cats' anal pouches and packed into zebu horns which are then sealed with leather ready for export.

C'est icy la figure de l'animal qui porte le musc dans une petite bourse entre le nombril et les pieds.

that many ships refused to carry it in case it escaped, sullying the rest of the cargo and entrancing the crew. It is a very special aphrodisiac, so close chemically to human testosterone that we can detect microscopic traces of it in a perfume. Scientists are now suggesting that we may have special musk receptors in our olfactory cavity. Elephants certainly find it erotic. The art of abhyanga, in which female elephants are massaged with musk ointment to make them more sexually alluring to male elephants, is still practised in India.

Musk was unknown outside the Far East until the sixth century AD, but in the following centuries it became one of the main luxuries brought by the Arabs from China along with silk, camphor and spices. Today, it remains one of the most important ingredients in perfumery, used in its natural or synthetic form in about 90 per cent of all fine fragrances. Perfumers maintain that nothing can capture the finesse of the real thing, but there are now over 80 synthetic types of musk available, in view of which it seems unforgivable to continue persecuting the deer.

A watercolour of a musk deer from the Jesuit *Voyage au Siam* of 1686. The musk pouch is on the deer's abdomen.

Synthetics

Perfumers are often at pains to let you know that none of the great perfumes of this century could have been created without synthetics, that synthetics open up whole new vistas in the realm of perfumery and that they have had an undeservedly bad press. They are right, of course, but in my view, synthetics are a mixed blessing. The world is certainly a richer place for Chanel No 5 and the brilliancy of its fatty aldehydes, but is it any better for detergents smelling of crude, synthesized pine or malls piped with ersatz pizza and coffee aromas to induce shoppers to stop and snack?

The fact is that synthetics are in a continuous process of refinement. Maybe the time will come when a laboratory-created rose will smell like the real thing, but at present, nature's roses win and how. Secondly, the relative crudeness of some synthetics mean they act like olfactory sledgehammers, and often they predominate too much in modern perfumery. The powerful klaxons of synthetic musks and blackcurrant are what assail the nose in the florientals of the mid- to late 1980s. For me, they have none of the subtlety of nature, but for many perfume wearers they are incredibly desirable, and have proved very popular. It's all a matter of taste, and there is no doubt that synthetics have changed tastes throughout the twentieth century.

When you inhale the odour from a favourite rose, you don't imagine that you are sampling nature's equivalent of a beaker of chemicals. But this is what a 'rose' actually means in terms of its scent. Nature's perfumes *are* chemicals, and many synthetic ingredients are identical to those found in nature.

There are two kinds of perfume materials classed as synthetics: isolates from nature and true synthetics. Isolates are individual chemicals separated out from the cocktails that are natural essential oils. They were first isolated in the mid-nineteenth century. True synthetics are produced by chemical reactions in the laboratory, often from coal tar and petroleum. The latter can be copies of substances found in nature or completely new creations, never smelt before. It is here that synthetics come into their own. Some of them are extraordinary and sophisticated discoveries that are among the most expensive ingredients. The vivid green top notes of Fidji by Guy Laroche, for example, are due to hexenylsalicylates, an unromantic name for a superb aroma that was invented at the same time as the fragrance.

In addition, some natural essential oils cannot be extracted in sufficient quantities from the plant to make a perfume, like lily-of-the-valley and lilac, and in this case, it is thanks to synthetics that we can smell them in the bottle at all. Another huge advantage is that synthetics can be used to replace animal extracts, important in today's ecologically aware world (not all synthetic musks, by the way, are are strong as the 1980s ones). The Nobel Prize for chemistry has been awarded to a scientist at wholesale fragrance company Firmenich for work mainly concerned with synthesizing musk and civet odours. This gives some idea of the level of sophistication required to produce new synthetics.

The great perfumer Ernest Beaux, who created Chanel No 5 in 1921, gives a idea of just how revolutionary synthetics have been: 'Up to the industrial realization of vanillin, heliotropin, coumarin and Musk Baur, the formulae were very simple and to a perfumer nowadays would seem naïve and humdrum. We rang the changes on rose, geranium, bois de rose, patchouli, clove, bergamot, neroli, petitgrain, lavender . . . the classic infusions, the resins. . . All perfumes, moreover, had a faint fatty note in common, to which one became accustomed; they were not very stable and deteriorated at the end of a certain time.'

Synthetics have allowed the flowering of mass-market perfumery, because many are much cheaper than essential oils. Producing natural essential oils is labour-intensive;

flowers have to be picked by people. A bad harvest means the price of a flower essence rockets, and bad weather can mean that the quality goes down, whereas the quality of a synthetic can be rigidly controlled. And you need never run out of chemicals, whereas someone else can buy up all the tuberose, for example, for their company, leaving you without enough for your new creation. All of these factors make synthetics very attractive to the perfumer.

Take Bulgarian rose, a very expensive ingredient which can therefore only be included in the costliest fine fragrances. What does a

Musk pods are cut away from the animals and sealed by the merchants with their characteristic wax seal. Nevertheless, the musk is nearly always adulterated to increase the weight of the pod and hence the price. These pods still bear the hairs from the animal's abdomen.

perfumer do if it is called for in his cheap, mass-market scent? Fake it. One of the main components of rose is citronellol, which is also found in the mosquito repelling plant, citronella. Of course, citronella does not smell like Bulgarian rose. It contains huge amounts of citronellol blended with other aromatic chemicals. Bulgarian rose contains much less, blended with a quite different roster of aromatics.

Herein lies one of the fascinating secrets of fragrant plants. Every plant

perfume is a bouquet of a few key aromatic chemicals, many of which also appear in other plants or even in animals. For example, indole is an essential part of jasmine. It is also found in other flowers, including orange blossom, tuberose and wallflowers, and, in a slightly different form, in animal excrement. Overpowering in excrement, it adds a sensual tang of flesh to jasmine. It's all a matter of quantity and the individual recipe of each aroma-cocktail. From these simple building blocks nature mixes a vast diversity of odours.

Back to the problem of recreating Bulgarian rose. The perfumer can

It is the dispenser's job to weigh out the formulae for perfumes.

extract citronellol much more cheaply and in greater abundance from the citronella plant than from the rose. But this is not the only key aroma in rose – there is also geraniol, usually extracted from geranium and palma rose, where it occurs in large quantities. Put these two together with a couple of other chemicals and the perfumer has his cheap and cheerful rose.

But it's not as easy as that. This lab rose never smells identical to the real thing. Most essential oils contain dozens, sometimes hundreds, of ingredients. Some are present only as traces at concentrations as small as 0.0001 per cent, but they might add an essential element to the rose's smell. A scientist can delineate the skeleton of a rose's smell, but he cannot reproduce the complexity of the fully-fleshed rose.

This may change. In the 1930s, scientists had isolated about half a dozen of the constituents of jasmine essential oil. Today, they know of several hundred, though 2–3 per cent of the oil is still not identified. It is liquid gas chromatography together with related analysis technologies that have made this knowledge possible.

Chromatography is a method of analysis whereby most chemicals in an essential oil can be separated out and pictured on a kind of graph. These scent maps are a bit like X-rays, allowing the inner working of a fragrance to be visualized. The liquid to be analysed is injected into a tube and progressively heated up to 200°C (390°F). Each chemical in it vaporizes at a precise temperature, and as they do so it is recorded on the tube, leaving the 'map'. Scientists can now go to a computer library that lists which chemicals evaporate at which temperatures, allowing them to identify most of the constituents of an essential oil.

There is another technique which has revolutionized fragrance in recent years: headspace analysis. When you smell a rose alive on the stem, it is quite different from the bottled rose. This is due partly to what perfumer Edmond Roudnitska calls 'the agony of the flower' as it dies. Its chemical composition begins to change the moment it is cut, just as the human body's does the moment it begins to die. Also, the heat or solvent used in the extraction process changes the

Headspace analysis analyses the scent of the living flower and aims to reproduce it in the flacon. The growing flower is covered with a sealed glass bottle and the air pumped out. Next, pure air is pumped in and the blossom releases its perfume into this naturally.

chemical balance of the rose and hence its smell.

Headspace analysis is basically an analysis of the living flower's bouquet. What looks like a space-helmet is strapped on to the growing flower and, after a while, the scented air collected in the helmet is taken back to the laboratory and analysed using chromatography to see just where it differs from the extracted essential oil. This allows for fine-tuning of a fragrance to bring it closer to the living flower. Living flower technology, as it is known, was developed by wholesale fragrance company IFF in New York. Dr Mookherjee, who pioneered the technique, describes it as 'touching the feet of God'. It allows us to re-create nature-identical scents. Living flower technology is used in fragrances like Prescriptives' Calyx and Yves Saint Laurent's Champagne.

Ernest Beaux said: 'For perfume, the future is above all in the hands of chemistry.' Already, there are industrial plants dedicated to producing just one synthetic material year after year. All modern highly commercialized perfumes contain a significant amount of synthetics, either as fragrance notes or fixatives. When we read about a scent having 'notes of rose, sandalwood and violet' it could mean that these notes are natural or synthetic. No one is going to sell their fragrance by telling us that it contains phenyl ethanol and damascenone. Aldehydes are the only synthetics that have received public acceptance as an exciting modern note.

But the day may come when the fields of flowers that the idea of fragrance conjures up may be almost totally replaced by genetically cloned essential oils cultivated in laboratories. It's just one more example of our culture's abandonment of reality in place of its virtual equivalent.

The Symphony of Scent

Perfumers often compare themselves to composers and a perfume to a piece of music. Like a symphony, a perfume has a beginning, a middle and an end, divided into three movements. What divides it up is the different rate of evaporation of its ingredients. The first movement is the introduction, the lightweight notes that sprint out of the bottle and into your nose, giving you an initial impression of the scent. They are called top notes or head notes. The second movement is the slower-to-evaporate heart or middle notes. They elaborate the main theme of the piece, sustained over several hours. Finally, the base notes appear. With their slow rate of evaporation, they can last all day, or for several days.

All the notes, however, are in the air from the beginning, and this makes the scent harder to control than a piece of music. A young trainee perfumer once described the creation of a new scent to me as like 'writing music in smoke'. The heart notes can usually be smelt very soon after the fragrance is applied. As the top notes evaporate to nothing, they develop and become stronger. Again, the base notes can be detected faintly early on, but it is as the other notes die away that they come to the fore, a deep chord that strengthens when the others have long gone.

It was the nineteenth-century perfumer Pièsse who first described perfume in terms of music. He devised a scheme where different odours were assigned to different musical notes on a scale. At the top of the scale were the tinkling Sugar-Plum Fairy notes of lavender, peppermint and pineapple; at the bottom the bass notes of patchouli, vanilla and resins like benzoin. He explained that there is an octave of odours as there are octaves in music, and that they must be combined in the right chords to be harmonious. The musical terminology is still used for scent.

Fixatives, which can be base notes like animal ingredients or unscented ingredients, are important because they have a slow rate of evaporation and slow down the evaporation of the whole, binding the scent together. Without proper fixing, you would smell each individual essential oil separately, as each has a different, specific rate of evaporation. So, for example, one minute the fragrance would be all rose, the next all jasmine. Too many fixatives, however, and a fragrance can seem flat.

The chemical structure of the ingredients affects the impression they give. Heavy fragrances, for example contain ingredients like musks, sandalwood, patchouli and labdanum, which are related to crystals, and give a compact, heavy effect to the scent.

Top notes	Heart notes	Base notes
Top notes tend to be green notes like crushed leaves, or citrus notes (also known as hesperides notes), fruits, herbs and light spring flowers. Typically, they fade after thirty minutes or so.	These are mostly floral notes with some spices and woody notes. They define the essential central character of a fragrance. On average, they last for 2–4 hours.	Also known as the 'dry down', these are the voluptuous animal notes, spices, resins, woods etc. Chypres and orientals are so rich in base notes that they are usually strong from the very beginning.
Lemon	Jasmine	Amber
Mandarin	Rose	Musk
Peach	Lily-of-the-valley	Oakmoss
Orange	Carnation	Vanilla
Lime	Ylang-ylang	Tonka bean
Bergamot	Tuberose	Orris
Pineapple	Orchid	Cinnamon
Cassis	Lilac	Sandalwood
Aldehydes	Geranium	Cedarwood
Coriander	Clove	Benzoin
Lavender	Neroli	Styrax
Pine	Gardenia	Leather notes
Vetiver	Freesia	Labdanum
		Patchouli

A badly-conceived fragrance has no harmony. Either the three levels are quite separate and don't work well together, or else they all jumble together without progression. Balance is everything, and roundness or 'volume' is a key characteristic of a well-constructed scent. When a scent has roundness, it has body and a coherent theme, discernible from top to bottom, even as the head, heart and base notes vary in their preponderance.

In individual fragrances, some notes that are described as typically top notes or heart notes can sometimes develop later or last longer because the particular composition is designed to slow their evaporation.

Just as a symphony is built round chords, so a fragrance is built of accords. Accords are a group of ingredients that harmonize together to give a new odour, more than and different to the sum of its parts.

From Perfume to Eau de Toilette

Although we call all alcohol-based fragrances 'perfumes', for the perfumer only the 'extrait' or pure perfume deserves the title. An extrait is the highest concentration of fragrance oils in alcohol, typically at a concentration of 15–40 per cent. Anything more diluted is classified as an 'eau' or water and, in fact, contains a certain amount of distilled water mixed with the alcohol. An eau de parfum contains typically 10–20 per cent of fragrance; an eau de toilette 8–10 per cent; an eau de Cologne 3–5 per cent, and an eau fraîche about 3 per cent.

The more alcohol in a fragrance, the lighter the effect. Often, a perfumer will change the balance of the eau de parfum or eau de toilette version of an extrait in line with this, so that it has recognizable traits of the extrait, but has fresher, cologne top notes. A few fragrances, notably Estée Lauder's Youth Dew, are diluted not in alcohol but in oils, which was the method used in ancient cultures.

In addition, modern fragrances usually also contain anti-oxidants as preservatives and a sunscreen to protect the fragrance from ultra-violet light, which alters the smell.

FRAGRANCE FAMILIES

Fragrances are divided into families, each headed by a great classic of its type. But just like actual family trees, they are often interrelated. In practice, this means some fragrances could be classed as belonging to more than one family. Knowing the family traits means you can be guided towards the type you will probably like at the fragrance counter. The fragrance wheel on page 61 provides an easy reference.

Floral family

This is the largest family, characterized by the predominance of heady flower notes. Classic of the genre are Houbigant's Quelques Fleurs of 1912 and Patou's Joy (1935). Florals can either centre on a single flower note like Diorissimo (1956 – lily-of-the-valley) or Chlöe (1975 – tuberose), or a bouquet like Nina Ricci's L'Air du Temps (1948) and Giorgio (1981).

Tuberose being gathered in India. The snowy trumpets of the tuberose emit an extraordinary scent like lilies dipped into clotted cream. Traditionally, they were the symbol of voluptuousness and young girls were forbidden to smell them in case they fell into a trance of voluptuous intoxication from which they could not easily escape. They are used in oriental and floral fragrances.

Aldehydic florals Aldehydes were first used to audacious effect in Chanel No 5 (1921), since when they have typified French fragrances. They amplify the top notes, bringing a champagne sparkle to a fragrance. Floral aldehydes include Lanvin's Arpège (1927), Mme Rochas (1960), Je Reviens by Worth (1932), Rive Gauche by Yves Saint Laurent (1971) and L'Interdit by Givenchy (1957).

Green florals smell of meadows, newly cut grass, leaves, rising sap and the light, limpid flower notes of spring. The first was Vent Vert by Balmain, created in 1945. Others include Fidji by Guy Laroche (1966), Givenchy III (1970), Ivoire by Balmain (1980) and Giò by Armani (1992).

Fruity florals: Calyx by Prescriptives (1987), Sunflowers by Elizabeth Arden (1993), Diamonds and Sapphires by Elizabeth Taylor (1993), Jean-Paul Gaultier (1993), Escape by Calvin Klein (1991).

Fresh florals (with citrus notes or the new 'transparent' flower notes): Anaïs Anaïs by Cacharel (1979), Flore by Caroline Herrera (1994), Eau d'Issey by Issey Miyake (1992).

Woody florals (with woody base notes): Chanel No 19, Safari by Ralph Lauren (1990), White Linen by Estée Lauder (1978).

Sweet florals: Blue Grass by Elizabeth Arden (1935), Gardenia Passion by Annick Goutal (1989), Eau Cuivrée by Montana (1994).

The orientals

Orientals are typically voluptuous, musky, spicy and exotic, melting into the flesh. The French call this family 'ambre' or amber. Classic orientals are Shalimar (1925) and Samsara (1989) by Guerlain, Opium by Yves Saint Laurent (1977) and Youth Dew by Estée Lauder (1952). The two biggest

subdivisions are florientals and spicy orientals.

Florientals first appeared in 1980s and are powerful but also flowery. They include Joop! by Joop! (1987), Panthère by Cartier (1986) and Spellbound by Estée Lauder (1992).

Spicy orientals, popular in the 1990s, are rich in culinary spices. They include Comme des Garçons (1994), Angel by Thierry Mugler (1992), Feminité du Bois by Shiseido (1992) and Old Spice (1937).

Fruity florientals: Poison by Dior (1985), Casmir by Chopard (1991).

Fruity orientals: Roma by Laura Biagiotti (1988), Moschino (1987).

Animal orientals: Obsession by Calvin Klein (1985), Egoïste by Chanel (1990).

Sweet orientals: Must de Cartier (1981), Donna Karan (1992).

The lavender fields of Provence yield one of the most universally beloved fragrances. Lavender comes from the Latin *lavare*, meaning to wash. Its pure, serene odour is part of the key accord in fougère fragrances but it also provides an herbaceous note in chypres and a feeling of the outdoors to some florals like Elizabeth Arden's Blue Grass, which contains English lavender. English lavender produces the finest oil.

Chypres

This is a highly original group of fragrances based on the contrast between bergamot-type top notes and mossy base notes. They are often strong, spicy and powdery, with resins in the base. There are almost as many masculine chypre fragrances as feminine. The name comes from Coty's Chypre of 1917, a bouquet of orange, geranium, spices and oakmoss, and a fragrance so individual it inspired a whole family of perfumes. Classic chypres include Ysatis by Givenchy (1984), Miss Dior by Dior (1947), Coriandre by Jean Couturier (1973) and Paloma Picasso (1984). The biggest subdivisions within the chypre family are the animal chypres and the floral chypres.

Animal chypres (with animal and sometimes leather base notes) include

Guerlain's Samsara is an oriental, a blend of rose (bottle), vanilla (bottle outline) and sandalwood (background).

Cabochard by Madame Grès (1958), Cuir de Russie by Chanel (1924), Scandal by Lanvin (1931), Jolie Madame by Balmain (1953), Polo by Ralph Lauren (1978) and Insensé by Givenchy (1993).

Floral chypres: Crêpe de Chine by Millot (1925), Ma Griffe by Carven (1946), Montana (1986), Knowing by Estée Lauder (1988).

Fruity chypres: Mitsouko by Guerlain (1919), Femme by Rochas (1944), Champagne by Yves Saint Laurent (1993).

Sweet chypres: Shocking by Schiaparelli (1937), Intimate by Revlon (1955), Aromatics Elixir by Clinique (1972).

Fresh chypres: Diorella by Dior (1972), Eau Parfumée by Bulgari (1992), CK1 by Calvin Klein (1994), Eau Sauvage by Dior (1966), Fahrenheit by Dior (1988).

Green chypres: Charlie by Revlon (1973), Alliage by Estée Lauder (1972), Boucheron Pour Homme (1991).

Fougères

Fougère is the French word for 'fern', a fantasy accord as ferns have no real fragrance. As the name suggests, these scents have a fresh, erotic, woodland scent, with aromatic, often lavender-accented top notes with an element of coumarin (the smell of fresh-mown hay), and a base of oakmoss, patchouli and labdanum. Originally a family of women's fragrances, headed by the classics Fougère Royale by Houbigant (1882) and Guerlain's Jicky (1889), they have developed into a mainly masculine family. There are two main subdivisions in the fougère family, floral fougères and leather fougères

Floral fougères: Canoë by Dana (1935), Wrappings by Clinique (1990), Parfum d'Eté by Kenzo (1992), Givenchy III (1970).

Leather fougères (with leather, tobacco and animal accents): Minotaure by Paloma Picasso (1992), Brut by Fabergé (1964), Tabac Blond by Caron (1919).

Woody fougères: Tuscany by Aramis (1985), Paco Rabanne Pour Homme (1973), Dunhill Edition (1986).

Spicy fougères: Alliage by Estée Lauder (1969), Jules by Dior (1980), Kouros by Yves Saint Laurent (1981).

Fresh fougères (with citrus notes): Eau d'Hadrien by Annick Goutal (1981), Ô de Lancôme (1969), English Lavender by Yardley (1770).

Green fougères: Cool Water by Davidoff (1988), Drakkar Noir by Guy Laroche (1982).

Ozonic fragrances

This is the newest fragrance category, defined by the inclusion of the fantasy note 'ozone', which indicates a watery, limpid feeling, or the algae-laden tang of sea air. Ozone notes had a humble beginning, added to detergents to give them that 'good morning' freshness. Ozone notes appear in New West by Aramis (1988), Dune by Dior (1992), Eden by Cacharel (1994) and Escape by Calvin Klein (1991).

The fragrance wheel shows how perfumes can be grouped into four main families. Within each family, the two main sub-divisions are shown in the middle ring, with smaller family units on the outer ring.

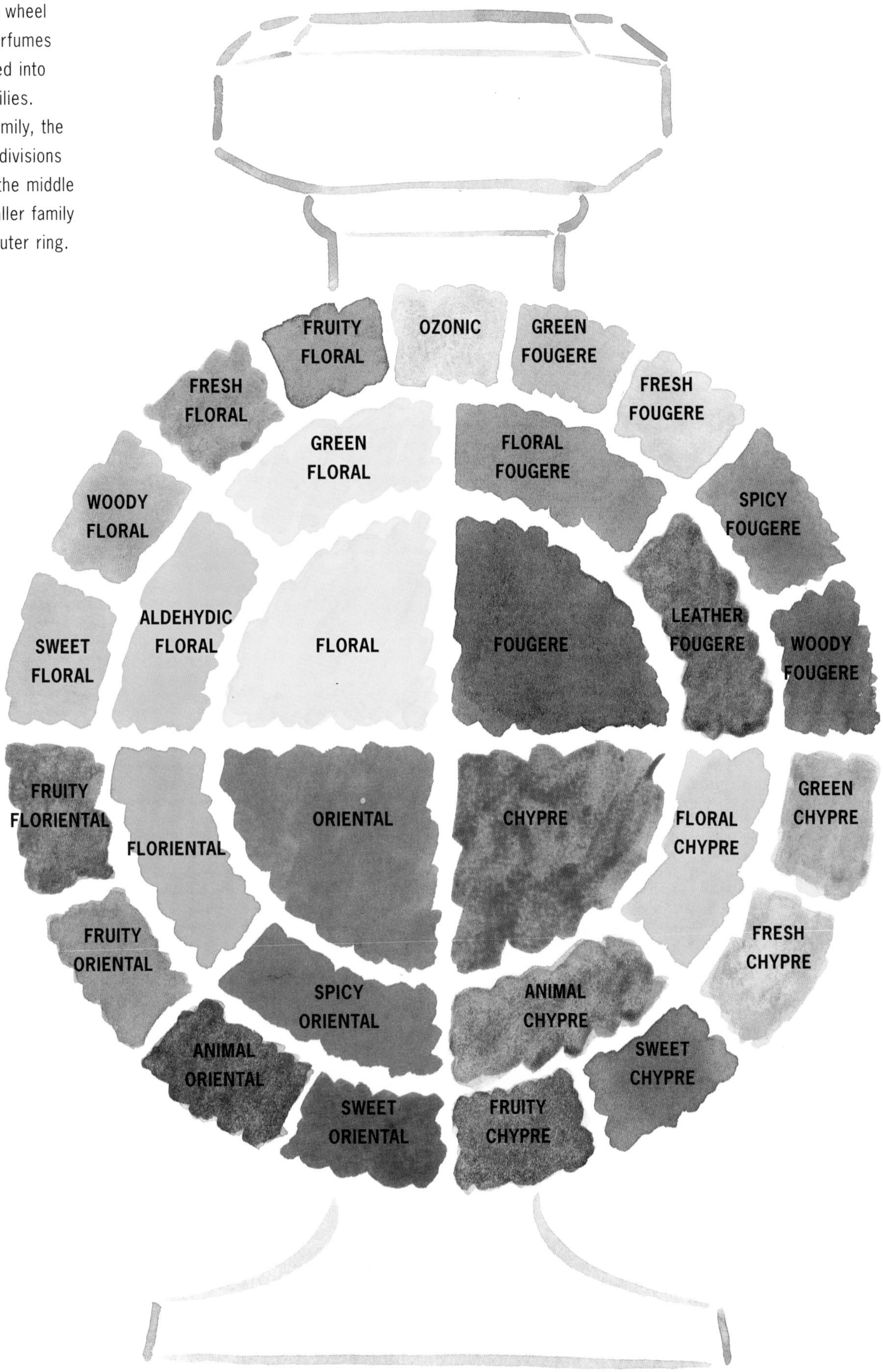

FRUITY FLORAL

OZONIC

GREEN FOUGERE

FRESH FLORAL

FRESH FOUGERE

GREEN FLORAL

FLORAL FOUGERE

WOODY FLORAL

SPICY FOUGERE

ALDEHYDIC FLORAL

FLORAL

FOUGERE

LEATHER FOUGERE

WOODY FOUGERE

SWEET FLORAL

FRUITY FLORIENTAL

ORIENTAL

CHYPRE

FLORAL CHYPRE

GREEN CHYPRE

FLORIENTAL

FRUITY ORIENTAL

FRESH CHYPRE

ANIMAL CHYPRE

SPICY ORIENTAL

ANIMAL ORIENTAL

SWEET CHYPRE

SWEET ORIENTAL

FRUITY CHYPRE

The Art of the Perfumer

Just as a musician needs a good ear and a painter a good eye, so a perfumer needs a good nose. In fact, the casual term for a perfumer in the industry *is* 'nose'. Some perfumers say that being able to tell not only that a particular phial of lavender essence comes from Grasse in the south of France but also whose field it comes from is a gift. Others, however, insist that their olfactory organ is 'no longer than anyone else's', as one put it, just better trained and more highly aware. In any case, the nose itself is only one part of their talent. The rest lies in imagination, olfactory memory, commercial sensibility, and understanding of chemistry. Perfumers are essentially artists in chemistry.

The analogy between music and fragrance runs deep. Not only does the perfumer see himself as a composer of scents, but traditionally he sat down to work at a special desk called an organ, because its shape was similar to that of a church organ. Instead of keys and stops, he was surrounded on three sides by rising ranks of extracts in little bottles. A century ago, there were about 150 ingredients for him to work with. Today, there are around 600–700 natural extracts and over 4,000 synthetic ones. In addition, he will have a large number of speciality bases, which are ready-made accords of synthetics and natural oils, some classics, some very new, produced by one of the big four fragrance companies to secret recipes. These speciality bases are the building blocks of many modern perfumes. Some ingredients

In the laboratory are found the thousands of ingredients, natural and synthetic, that must be weighed out with great precision to make a fragrance. In the foreground, metal clips hold fans of scent strips. These are sprayed with different perfumes and sniffed throughout the day to assess the development over time of new fragrances.

which are very viscous are kept in ovens, others which are very volatile in refrigerators, but the majority of those an individual nose regularly uses from this huge arsenal will be ranged round his desk in the laboratory. Few perfumers nowadays work at an organ.

A perfumer usually works between an office and a laboratory. The office is for meeting clients, assessing scents and doing paperwork. Some trials of the scent he is working on will usually be on the desk in code-numbered bottles and a fan of paper scent strips clipped into a metal holder will allow him to test the different versions away from the scent of his own skin. The perfumer starts the day by exercising his nose the way a musician practises scales. In his case, he will identify the ingredients in a number of sample bottles the lab techicians have laid out for him. Next door, in the laboratory, the bottles of ingredients will be stacked and it is here that the lab technicians weigh out the formulae.

Every industry has its own patois, and perfumery is no exception. A perfume is referred to as the '*jus*' or juice, except at Guerlain, where they humorously call it '*la soupe*'. The average perfume contains anything from 30 to several hundred ingredients.

Once the perfumer has decided on the composition of his trial perfume, the ingredients are weighed and the formula recorded in parts per thousand, for example, 50 parts jasmine, 90 parts rose, 3 parts musk, and so on. He will then play around with this core formula daily, experimenting and improving it over months. It can take many years of daily grind to perfect a perfume. A successful modern perfume has to fight to be noticed in a saturated market of thousands, most of which come and go within a few years. Because of this, striking top notes that grab the consumer's interest have become a crucial strategy. But the opposite strategy can also work well. Many people are drawn to familiar, reassuring smells.

Perfumers often have a signature which they write into almost every scent: a favourite accord they may 'play' throughout a fragrance or allow a brief but familiar appearance. All Guerlain fragrances, for example, include an accord known as the Guerlainade, and it is this which makes a Guerlain perfume so instantly recognizable. All have their own palette of odours, like a painter's palette, and Jean-Paul Guerlain has said that his grandfather, the famous

A close-up of one side of a perfumer's organ, showing a small number of the ingredients at his disposal. Not only will he have rose, for example, but maybe twenty different rose oils and absolutes, some already mixed into speciality bases by one of the fragrance wholesale companies.

Jacques Guerlain, composed his 50 or so fragrances from a palette of only a hundred ingredients.

In the first half of this century, there were still a substantial number of perfumers working freelance or contracted to one of the big fashion houses. They had a great deal of freedom as artists, and the luxury of time, producing maybe one fragrance every four or five years. Nowadays, the perfumer does not have that luxury. Only a handful work for one fashion house or a small, independent perfumers; the rest are all within the huge international flavour and fragrance companies that dominate the market. Over 90 per cent of all fine fragrances come from these companies where scientists, perfumers and marketing people work together producing everything from high-quality scents through the fragrance in your detergent to the flavourings in cigarettes, soft drinks and paper handkerchiefs. Fine fragrances form a relatively small part of their business – about 20 per cent. Four multinational companies dominate the fine fragrance market: IFF (International Flavours and Fragrances) based in the US, the Anglo-Dutch company Quest International, and Givaudan-Roure and Firmenich, both Swiss companies.

Until recently trainee perfumers took up to ten years to learn their trade, usually at the perfumery schools within one of these companies. Both perfumers training in fine fragrance and those who will scent products like household cleaners and shopping-mall aromas are highly skilled. As Mlle Marin, who headed the Givaudan-Roure school at Grasse, puts it: 'Fine fragrance is poetry, household fragrance is prose – both demand special talents.' There are three main stages to training.

First, the young perfumers memorize the vast vocabulary of odours, a process that they will continue to perfect throughout their lives. They do this by association, cleverly making use of smell's powerful ability to reawaken memories. If when they smell patchouli they think of the damp leaves at the edge of a lake they knew as a child, this is what they write in their notebooks. These highly personal 'association notebooks' will enable them to memorize a huge library of odours. Next, the students learn the building blocks of fragrance, the classic accords which smell not of their constituents but quite different, more than the sum of their parts – like the jasmine-rose accord. At the same time they are learning about the science and rates of evaporation of the various oils. In the second stage they are given formulae – but no proportions – for all the main families, chypres, fougères, colognes, and learn to compose these to their tutor's satisfaction. As Mlle Marin says: 'Perfume is proportion, proportion, proportion.'

At this point, when the training is over, the young perfumer is despatched to work in all the various parts of the processing plant and weighing formulae

Jacques Guerlain assessing a trial scent on a fan of scent strips. He is one of the greatest perfumers of the twentieth century, creating the great Guerlain classics L'Heure Bleue, Mitsouko and Shalimar, among others.

Jacques Polge is one of a handful of perfumers who are still employed by individual houses, in his case Chanel. Polge, seen here among the roses in Grasse, is the guardian of Chanel No 5 and creator of Chanel's Coco and Egoïste for men. 'I don't consider perfume as an art,' he says, 'but it's not that I mind being an artisan. I adore being an artisan.'

in the compounding rooms, for several months in each area. Finally comes the exam. The student is given a fragrance, unmarked, and told to copy it, just as painters used to learn by first copying the Old Masters. When the original and the copy cannot be distinguished in double blind tests, it is taken it to the head perfumer. If the head is satisfied, the trainee becomes a junior perfumer. Sadly, many of the perfume schools have recently closed or greatly reduced the length of training.

The fine fragrance perfumers are specialists within the company who won't be concocting a new toilet bowl freshener one day and an eau de toilette the next. They work in great secrecy to briefs for clients who want to launch a scent, be they a fashion house, a celebrity or a shop, as in the case of Giorgio. This means that while the perfumer is a creative artist, he or she is one who works within tight commercial constraints. Often the brief is vague: 'I need something for the modern woman with a strong sense of herself but a warm heart.' What, after all, does a modern woman with a strong sense of herself smell like?

But as fragrance is all about emotion and mood, impressions like this can be gradually translated into formulae by the nose, who will probably produce between 50 and several hundred trials, some only subtly different from each other, others radically so, before honing it down to two or three options that are felt to be strong contenders. Sometimes the perfumer will feel strongly about one trial, the marketing people about another and the client about a third. At this stage, they are tested – anonymously – on a batch of women to see which one consumers prefer. The final choice, however, is up to the client.

Female noses

Women have been significant in the art of perfumery since the most ancient times. Priestesses at the pre-Biblical temples of the Middle Eastern goddesses are the first recorded perfumers, and women retained their reputation as perfumers in Bibilical times: 'This will be the way of the king . . . and he will take your daughters to be perfumers.' (1 Sam., 8:11, 13).

In modern times, women worked in the fields, their delicate hands less likely to bruise the flower-crop than those of men, but they were largely excluded from the creative work. Nevertheless, some of the great perfumes of the century have been created by women.

Going right back to the 1940s, one of the most innovative scents of the century, Balmain's Vent Vert, was created by a woman, Germaine Cellier. This modern genius also concocted Jolie Madame and Madame Balmain for Balmain, and Fracas and the great Bandit for

Edmund Roudnitska is another formidable talent in perfumery, creator of Madame Rochas, Diorissimo and Dior's ground-breaking Eau Sauvage, among others.

Below: Germaine Cellier, one of the few female noses in the first half of the twentieth century.

Robert Piguet. Annette Louit of L'Oréal has overseen all the best-selling Cacharel fragrances, including Anaïs Anaïs and Loulou, while Jean-Charles Brosseau's Ombre Rose was created by Christine Caron. Josephine Catapano, 'the first perfumer to really put American fragrance on the map,' according to New Yorker Sophia Chodosz-Grosjman, did Fidji for Guy Laroche and Novell for Revlon. Herself one of the most gifted noses of the 1980s and 1990s, Grosjman has given us Calvin Klein's Eternity, Yves Saint Laurent's Paris and Champagne, Prescriptives' Calyx and Lancôme's Trèsor, among others.

Frenchwoman Annick Goutal has worked on some of the most beautiful and original scents of the last decade for her eponymous company. Against all the odds, she set up her own company rather than working within one of the multinationals (though she has since been bought out by Groupe du Louvre). The individuality of the scents she has therefore been able to produce has made them the favourites of cognoscenti all over the world.

Chapter Three

Bottling Allure

Ancient bottles thousands of years old show that perfumes have always merited luxurious containers. Every conceivable substance from ostrich eggs and semi-precious stones to porcelain and crystal has been used to encapsulate these evanescent elixirs. The designs also suggest how perfume has been used down the centuries. In the eighteenth century, scent-shovels, pomanders and bottles fashioned with a jeweller's art reveal how fragrance penetrated every corner of bourgeois existence. In our own century, perfume has been brought to the mass market, but not at the expense of exquisite flacons. Beautiful bottles are smart marketing, but since scent is as much a symbol as it is a fragrant substance, the importance of the bottle goes beyond the commercial to the roots of what perfume means.

DES CALRCES COTY

Ancient Amphorae

In ancient civilizations, many perfumes were as precious as liquid jewels and, as such, were stored in luxurious containers. At the same time, scent had many more functions and was used more liberally than today, and there are also hundreds of simple clay and stone flasks designed for its different everyday uses. Museums are full of what look like tiny terracotta vases called lekythoi, designed in fact to hold perfume oils. They usually have a slender handle and a very narrow neck, so that only a few drops of the liquid can be shaken out at a time.

The oldest known perfume containers come from the eastern Mediterranean, from Mesopotamia and Ancient Egypt, and date back at least 5,000 years. Alabaster, calcite and stone were the preferred materials because they are non-porous and keep the scent cool, preventing it from going off. Massive alabaster unguent jars were found in Tutankhamun's tomb (1350 BC), for example, still faintly fragrant after over 3,000 years. Earth and clay were also widely used, sculpted in the shape of people and animals, especially fish. Other materials used include ivory, bone, faience, porphyry, bronze and ostrich eggs, which are among the most ancient.

Ingenious designs were favoured. One, from about the seventh century BC, shows a kneeling woman holding a large jar with a frog squatting on the top. The scent is poured from the frog's mouth. Another bottle in ivory, from Lachish in Palestine, is of a standing woman, arms akimbo to form handles, with the top of a spoon emerging from her head. When the bottle was tilted, a few drops would drip onto the spoon, ensuring none of the valuable contents was wasted.

Left: A clay hedgehog scent bottle from Egypt dating from around the third century BC. Originally, this would have been stoppered with a plug of linen or wood.

Right: An alabaster alabastron from c.1500 BC. With its wide flat neck and rounded base, this albastron is a typical shape.

Many finds come from tombs. Perfumes were used in most of the Mediterranean cultures in preparing the bodies of the dead, and also served as funerary gifts. In Egyptian tombs, beautifully painted boxes are often found, divided into compartments each containing a different ointment pot. These were the portable dressing-tables of ancient times. From Queen

A green glass sand-core perfume bottle from the fifth century BC, one of many such bottles commonly found in the Mediterranean area. Almost all have coloured wavy or zig-zag threads, done by combing the hot glass.

Hetepheres' tomb, for example, comes a wooden toilette box with eight little alabaster jars and a copper spoon. Seven jars contained the seven traditional perfumes of Egypt, and the eighth held kohl. The lids are inscribed with the name of the scents, and a matching hieroglyph on the rim of the jar shows which lid belongs to which jar.

Small pots and vases, or amphorae, were for carrying on the person, hence their little looped handles so that they could be hung from a belt. Others with a little spout were for topping up oil lamps. The bigger pots were for oils used in cleaning the body. Large open alabaster vessels on high feet may have been for offering perfumed oils to guests at banquets, a tradition that continues today in many Islamic countries where guests are offered rosewater to refresh themselves.

Glass flacons start to appear in Egypt in the fifteenth century BC. Glass is perfect for storing perfume. It is light and, unlike terracotta, non-porous so the perfume doesn't evaporate through the bottle. The early vessels were cut from a solid piece of glass and then polished. By the fourth century BC small flasks of coloured glass had spread all along the Mediterranean coast. The Greek geographer and historian Strabo (*c*.60 BC–AD 20) was full of praise for the glass flacons of Diospolis (now Lod) in Palestine, which were coloured sapphire, hyacinth and ruby-red.

The Hebrews also had an advanced perfume culture, no doubt influenced by their exile in Egypt. Horn-shaped ivory vessels have been discovered that may have been the mysterious 'horn of oil' referred to in their coronation ceremonies: 'And Xadok the priest took the horn of oil from the tent and anointed Solomon' (1 Kings 1:39). Others have suggested that they were used for anointing the bodies of pregnant women.

Glass 'candlestick' bottles with a wide base and very long narrow neck were common in Palestine. Because they were mostly found in tombs, nineteenth-century scholars dubbed

A ninth- to tenth-century AD glass balm bottle from Iran.

them lacrimatoria, assuming they were intended for collecting the tears of the bereaved. However, recent sediment tests have revealed traces of olive oil, which was commonly used as a base for perfumes of the period, and they are now thought, rather more prosaically, to be scent bottles.

Perfume was not only used in funerary rites, but would have helped to purify the stench of decomposing flesh when relatives returned to visit the family burial chambers on certain festivals. Large vases of perfumes and spices were placed in cemeteries for the same reason: 'A flask of foliatum [prepared from spikenard] . . . stood in the cemetery and its smell was spreading' (Yalqut Shimoni, Gen 49).

The ancient Greeks took the art of clay pottery to its height. They stored perfumes in beautifully painted vases and flacons, again often shaped into animals like hedgehogs or ducks. A common motif was a sandalled foot, perhaps connected with the ritual of washing and anointing dusty feet. Another frequently used shape was the plemoche, a wide, lidded bowl with a rim folding inwards, which was placed on a high stand next to the bath and contained cheaper perfumes for use after bathing.

The aryballos is the typical Greek scent container. These were originally amphora-shaped but were later made in a wide variety of forms, like animal shapes, a Gorgon's head, or a woman's breast. Aryballoi were often round or pointed at the bottom, because they were designed to be hung from a hook or belt rather than stood on a surface. They usually had a wide, flat mouth but a very narrow neck which allowed

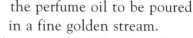

A Roman scent flask in blown glass. The body of the bottle represents the two-headed god Janus, after whom the month of January is named. One head is looking back over the old year, the other looking forward to the new.

the perfume oil to be poured in a fine golden stream.

The majority of Greek perfume vases came from Corinth, where the semi-industrial methods that were used meant that designs were often produced in a series of decreasing sizes, just as with modern commercial perfume bottles. Different designs may even have been produced to identify the different perfumes inside, in the same way as modern labels are used.

Not long after the birth of Christ, glass-blowing was discovered at Sidon on the coast of Syria. Soon glass bottles and pitchers were being blown all over the Roman Empire, even in the south of England. The most common shapes were animals, bunches of grapes and other fruit, shells and, above all, the ever-popular fish. From then on, throughout the period of Roman rule, glass was the favourite material for perfume bottles, and pearlescent flasks and vases of great beauty and simplicity were produced. The Romans also favoured hollowed-out jewels for carrying especially precious perfumes, while the Etruscans had carried perfumes pinned to their breasts in brooch-bottles.

Beyond the Mediterranean, scent was equally important, especially in religious and funerary rites. Huge bronze Chinese incense burners remain from the first millennium BC, and also pierced gold containers for holding in the hands during votive ceremonies. In pre-Columbian Mexico and Peru, both golden dishes and clay or terracotta pots were used to burn narcotic incenses in religious ceremonies.

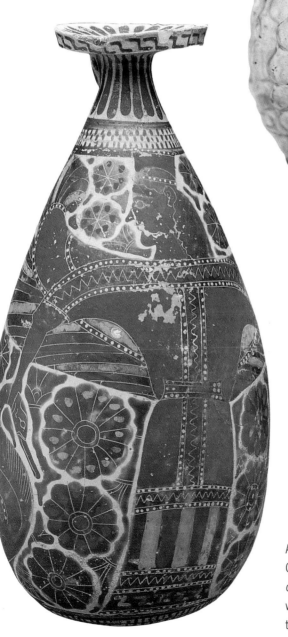

A beautifully painted Corinthian alabastron of c.600 BC showing a winged 'mistress of the animals'.

Early European Bottles

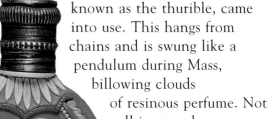

In the seven centuries or so leading up to our own, scent receptacles have witnessed wild flights of the imagination. Scent insinuated itself into everything and was stored in practically anything. Glass was important of course, but so were gold, silver, porcelain, semi-precious stones and shells. Even peach-stones, stoppered with ivory, were deftly turned into flacons. Long flutes of coloured glass designed to lie on their side were used for toilet waters in the eighteenth and nineteenth centuries. River mussels were polished to a mother of pearl shimmer, mounted in silver and filled with perfumes. A spring in a carved silver rose opens to reveal smelling salts in a nineteenth-century container from Edinburgh, Scotland. And little silk scent pouches were filled with powdered aromatics in the seventeenth century and secreted in a pocket, under a pillow or in the hem of a garment.

Two English scent bottles made by Josiah Wedgwood in the eighteenth century.

Scent survived the Dark Ages thanks to the Arabs and the Church. When St Augustine forbade all pleasures of the flesh in the fourth century AD, he happily exempted the fleshly pleasure of perfume. Incense had been much used by Hebrews, Egyptians, Greeks and Romans, but its use was proscribed during the early years of the Christian Church. It was gradually reintroduced, and by the thirteenth century censers were an essential part of every church. In the ninth century, the swung censor, known as the thurible, came into use. This hangs from chains and is swung like a pendulum during Mass, billowing clouds of resinous perfume. Not all incense-burners are swung, however. Two magnificent silver cranes in the treasury of Mainz cathedral were designed to stand on either side of the altar, with smoke hissing from their bills.

Perfume was not only a spiritual imperative but a magical amulet to ward off evil. Silver earrings, with hollow spheres containing a scrap of cloth soaked in perfume, were considered effective in warding off spells that entered by the ears even into the eighteenth century. Perfume was also used to keep the effluvia of disease at bay. The strangest scent-receptacles ever must surely be the false noses made of leather or papier mâché with a sponge soaked in aromatic vinegar in the tip. They came from the East via Venice and were worn by doctors to examine plague victims (hence the nickname 'quacks') until they were eventually denounced in 1720 by a French prelate who observed that they terrified patients.

While the Persians already had rosewater atomizers in the Middle Ages, the Western world used mainly solid perfumes until the seventeenth century. These were not applied to the skin but dangled in pierced balls of metal (pomanders) from the body. Like so much to do with perfume, pomanders came from the Middle East. The first recorded was presented to the crusader Emperor Frederick Barbarossa in 1174 by King Baldwin of Constantinople.

The word pomander is a contraction of the French *pomme d'ambre* ('apple of amber'). Their globe shape seems to have developed from the practice of rolling a melting mass of castoreum into a ball in the palms, then, when it had hardened, carrying it on a chain. Rosaries were originally scented, made of dried rosebuds or beads of hardened aromatic substances, and pomanders were often attached to them or else, from the sixteenth century, hooked decoratively on to clothes.

As the German name for them, bismapfel (from *bisam* – musk and *apfel* – apple), shows, pomanders were originally filled mainly with musk, and only later with ambergris. Musk was infinitely costly, weighed against gold, and so no expense was spared in the pomanders containing it. Most are in gold and silver, richly decorated, often with jewels which also had a prophylactic significance. Garnets, for example, were thought to protect the wearer from the plague and other fevers. These pomanders were worn round the neck, or hung from a belt; small ones were attached by a chain to a finger ring. Later pomanders open out like quartered apples to reveal slices, each filled with a different scent for different purposes. A sliding lid for each slice meant any one section could be opened at a time.

Actual perfume bottles were first made in the sixteenth

A sixteenth-century German pomander in gilded silver, with different sections for different scents, each engraved with the name of a scent: civet, ambre (ambergris), citroni (lemon), rosemarin and angelica. All these scents were thought to have medicinal qualities and to help keep diseases at bay.

century and reached a zenith in the seventeenth century, when most pieces were unique works of art commissioned by noblemen. Scent was always a status symbol, even more than now, and scent containers of all kinds were fashioned by court jewellers, goldsmiths and silversmiths into objects of great beauty and ingenuity. Many bottles were designed to be worn, others to be displayed on a table, and their value is shown by the fact that they were part of every Renaissance princeling's treasury. In the sixteenth century, every banquet table of note had a gold or silver rosewater fountain as its centrepiece, in which the guests could dabble their greasy fingers.

Pomanders began to go out of fashion in the seventeenth century to be replaced by smelling-boxes, which look rather like slim, elegant cigarette cases on the outside. In England, silver and gold smelling-boxes with pierced lids known as pouncet boxes had been known since Elizabethan times. In the eighteenth century, as liquid perfumes became commonplace, they became vinaigrettes, with a sponge soaked in perfumed vinegar tucked under a metal grille inside. Small enough to be secreted in a pocket or a muff, vinaigrettes could be opened and inhaled at any hint of the vapours or to quickly banish the noxious miasma that permeated eighteenth-century cities. In the mid-nineteenth century they were replaced by simpler glass and cut crystal smelling-bottles filled with 'smelling salts'.

Rooms, too, had to be fumigated and perfumed. Fume pots and scent-shovels were designed to carry smouldering coals smothered with pastilles of odorous pastes. Casting-jugs with pierced stoppers were an old English invention for sprinkling scent over rushes and linen. Perfume-burners or *brûle-parfums* appeared at the end of the sixteenth century as liquid perfumes and toilet waters came into use. Originally made of metal, some used a wick floating in perfumed oil, others consisted of a bowl with a pierced lid on a tripod, with a dish for a spirit flame underneath. They often look a bit like samovars. By the eighteenth century, painted porcelain *brûle-parfums* came in endless fanciful shapes. Meissen, the first Western company to crack the secret of making porcelain in 1710, was known for its cross-legged Buddhas blowing aromatic smoke from their grinning mouths.

Marco Polo had first brought back porcelain, the 'white gold', from China in the thirteenth century. In the West, it gave rise to a plethora of ornamental scent bottles and pot-pourri dishes in rococo designs. Pot-pourri was placed either in flat, open dishes or in painted vases with pierced lids, bulging with putti and moulded flowers. Many scent bottles took the form of statuettes like Girl Playing the Lyre, Pug Dog, Lover as Bird-Catcher, The Shepherdess, or a set of double bottles in the form of, to take one example, a monkey with a baby

From the English Girl in a Swing factory, this 1750s porcelain bottle shows a beau cajoling a blushing maiden. 'Le Moyen de Parvenir' (how to succeed) inscribed on the base indicates his intentions.

monkey on its back. Some of the best came from England.

Voltaire called the eighteenth century the 'century of smallness'. Perfume bottles lent themselves well to the aesthetic of daintiness. Just as popular as porcelain and glass were the bijou enamelled scent bottles, often in a teardrop shape and with gold settings, that came mostly from England. They were decorated with scenes from classical mythology, landscapes, pastoral idylls and baskets of fruit and flowers. It became fashionable to send your lover *'l'instant d'un moment'*: a scent bottle inscribed with a billet-doux message like 'Love & Wine'.

In what we would now recognize as rather a kitsch spirit, by the early nineteenth century porcelain bottles also sometimes took the form of automata, like a combination flacon and musical clock. The height of this capricious style is a Swiss pearl-studded perfume-pistol in Sotheby's collection. When the trigger is pulled, a set of gilded petals pops from the end of the barrel to release a squirt of scent. Even more bizarre were the *pisseuses à parfum* or perfume-pissers, tiny atomizers in the shape of women, usually half-naked and with their legs apart to reveal a small hole from which the perfume was sprayed.

In the seventeenth century the accoutrements of the toilette were packaged together in a box known as an étui. Inside would be essentials such as scissors, ear-spoons, penknives, combs and scent bottles. Eventually, étuis were made specially for fragile scent bottles. Toilette boxes or *caves à odeur* ('odour cellars') were popular. They held two or more bottles, a funnel and maybe a dish for mixing your own fragrance, and were designed to be taken travelling. Some looked rather like our hip flasks, while others came in the shape of a leather- or shagreen-bound book.

In the eighteenth century, the simpler étui metamorphosed into a nécessaire which contained, according to Charlotte, Duchess of Orléans, 'everything necessary for having tea, coffee and chocolate'. They also held scent bottles, powder boxes, vases for almond paste and all the paraphernalia of an elaborate make-up that could take hours to complete. Nécessaires made popular wedding gifts.

Bergamots, an eighteenth-century speciality of Grasse, were small boxes made from bergamot orange peel that was hardened until it had the texture of thin, stiffened leather. The fragrant boxes were then doused in bergamot and rose oil before being sold, usually as containers for scent bottles.

France did not become the centre of the perfume business until the seventeenth century. Until then, it was Italy, and above all Venice, gateway to the East, that held fragrant sway. Coloured glass bottles, especially of the millefiori or 'thousand flowers' design, were made in the sixteenth century at Murano in Venice to contain the new perfume oils. Then the Venetians discovered how to make a glass as clear as rock crystal, but much cheaper. Pure, transparent glass, something we now take for granted, was held to be especially beautiful, like diamonds above rubies.

Glass is ideal for storing perfume in all but one respect: it lets in light,

Nécessaires like this were popular eighteenth-century wedding presents.

A nineteenth-century Venetian glass smelling-salts bottle.

which alters the perfume over time. But it also allows the beauty of the scent itself to show through. As Edmund Launert puts it in his book *Perfume and Pomanders*: 'What could be more delightful to the eye than a row of glass bottles full of costly perfumes ranging in colour from pale sea green to deep amber?' The use of glass for scent bottles grew slowly in popularity until practically all scent bottles were of mass-produced glass by the end of the nineteenth century.

At the time, fragrance was mostly sold in cheap, often plain, bottles with gaudy labels, and decanted into toilette bottles at home. Many fragrance companies sold their perfumes in identical bottles, differentiated only by these big decorative labels. But at the beginning of the twentieth century, the great glass genius René Lalique, in partnership with perfumer François Coty, ushered in the modern era of perfume marketing, wedding fine fragrances to individual bottles that reflected the character or the name of each particular scent.

Lalique

The twentieth century may be the era of mass-produced bottles, but it has also seen some of the most inspired and exquisite flacons ever made. The century opened with the work of a genius who crafted some of the most beautiful artefacts ever to encapsulate perfume. René Lalique, born in 1860, began life as a jeweller, a profession at which he also excelled. He was one of the foremost exponents of the art nouveau style, producing sinuous dragonflies, scarabs, nymphs and peacocks in glowing enamels and semi-precious stones.

Towards the end of the nineteenth century he began to incorporate glass into his pieces, and in 1893 he used the lost wax method to make what was probably his first flacon, a unique piece in which a fish shimmers out of the shadowed depths of the bottle. In 1906, Lalique was approached by the young perfumer François Coty to design the bottles for his creations. Coty's plan was grand, but shrewd: 'Offer a woman the best product you can make and present it in a perfect container (beautiful, simple, but in the best possible taste), ask a reasonable price for it, and you will have a commercial proposition such as the world has never seen.'

Coty wanted to make luxury affordable, a philosophy that has worked for the perfume business ever since. Lalique's first flacon for him was

The exquisite Baiser d'un Faune ('Kiss of a Faun') designed by Lalique for Molinard in 1928. The fragrance formed a golden ring around the central medallion.

probably L'Effleurt de Coty in 1908. Like many of Lalique's bottles, it expresses the essence of fragrance. A swooning, naked female genie rises in a swirl of vapours and veils from curling honeysuckle petals, like the spirit of perfume itself.

Lalique's flacons capture the sensuality of scent, and his love of sinuous forms, garlands and tendrils evoke its invisible streams expanding up from the bottle. He favoured *demi-cristal* glass, which has a lower lead content than crystal. This gives the bottles a softer, warmer feel. The glass is often matt, opalescent and patinated, sometimes emerging into areas of brilliant transparency. The flacons are smoky, dreamy, sometimes with a wash of delicate colour, and figures and flowers emerge from the glass only to evaporate back into it. He also designed ambitious stoppers that swoop down like wings to hang on either side of the bottle in a mass of flowers, fruits or a trio of swallows.

The Lalique/Coty partnership was a great success, and Lalique went on to design at least sixteen flacons for Coty, among which are some of his most beautiful, like Au Coeur des Calices ('In the Heart of the Calyces'), L'Entraînement ('The Impulse') and Ambre Antique. Lalique also made bottles for many other perfumers, like Houbigant, Roger et Gallet, D'Orsay, Forvil, Arys and Molinard. One well-known collaboration was with Worth,

Fougères ('Ferns'), 1912, was designed as a toilette bottle. The central medallion is framed by stylized fern fronds, which also appear on the stopper.

for whom Lalique designed the skyscraper Je Reviens ('I Return') bottle (based on a Mies van der Rohe drawing of 1921) and the lovely frosted blue globe with transparent stars for Dans la Nuit ('In the Night'), among many others.

Arguably Lalique's most beautiful bottle was for Molinard's Baiser d'un Faune ('Kiss of a Faun'), in which a dancing faun and nymph kiss in the centre of the bottle. The scent is contained in a ring around this centrepiece. Created in 1928, it was inspired by Stéphane Mallarmé's poem *L'Après-midi d'un faune*, which was also set to music by Debussy and turned into a ballet. Lalique was often inspired by dancers, especially Loïe Fuller, who danced with veils on a glass floor lit from below, and Isadora Duncan. The set of Duncan toilette bottles is still made today to the original design by Cristal Lalique.

The beautiful La Belle Saison, designed for Houbigant in 1926, uses a similar idea to Fougères. Here, the stylized leaves radiating out from the central medallion to terminate in blossoms also resemble the sun rays of 'the beautiful season', the French name for the summer months. This effect is enhanced by the golden-yellow glow of the fragrance.

Lalique's designs were made affordable thanks to series production, in which a large number of small, artistic bottles could be turned out on a more sophisticated level than mass production. But he also created a great number of simpler, mass-produced bottles that are still worthwhile collector's pieces. Lalique's bottles carry special prestige among perfume-flacon collectors. Rare pieces have changed hands for tens of thousands of dollars, while others, like the Worth skyscraper, can be picked up in flea-markets for about US $50. Anyone thinking of venturing into collecting should read *Lalique Perfume Bottles* by American collectors Mary Lou and Glenn Utt (Crown, New York, 1990), which gives full details of verifying the Lalique marks and signature, and other useful information.

When Lalique died in 1945, his son Marc took over the firm and himself produced a number of famous flacons. Among these is perhaps the best-known bottle in the world, Nina Ricci's L'Air du Temps ('The Spirit of the Times') in 1951, with its billing doves on the stopper. He also created the bottle for Rochas' Femme, based on the shape of Mae West's hips. On Marc's death in 1977, the running of the firm passed to his daughter, Marie-Claude Lalique. She continued the Lalique association with Parfums Nina Ricci when she designed the bottle for their Nina in 1987. The glassmakers Pochet et du Courval, who exclusively produce perfume bottles, own the majority share in Lalique today.

A glass table centrepiece of around 1910 with a central *brûle-parfum*. The invisible perfume streaming from the bottle is visualized as a fountain of glass water with fanciful fish swimming in the spray. The 'water' jets out from the central *brûle-parfum* to the metal frogs at either side.

René Lalique's first commercial perfume-related designs were glass plate 'labels' that could be attached to plain mass-produced glass bottles. This was the basis of L'Effleurt, designed for François Coty in 1908, which later evolved into this complete bottle design. The pair of winged beetles that form the stopper recall Lalique's earlier jewellery designs.

Baccarat and Beyond

Lalique dominated the art of flaconnage in the first third of the century, but other beautiful bottles came notably from Cristalleries de Baccarat, who could be commissioned either to design and produce the flacons themselves, or to make them to other people's designs, as with Le Roy Soleil, designed by Salvador Dali.

Other beautiful designs came from the glass-maker Julien Viard and from artists known in other fields. Hector Guimard, who designed the art nouveau Paris metro stations, made bottles for the firm of Millot, and the cubist artist Fernand Léger for furriers Revillon. His abstract ripple of water frozen in glass for their Cantilène of 1948 was one of his experiments in bringing

poetry to everyday objects. Dali not only designed bottles and labels for couturier Elsa Schiaparelli, but launched his own perfume, Electricité, in the 1950s to an audience of astonished art critics. Later, in the 1980s, Parfums Salvador Dali was formed and produced bottles inspired by some of his earlier surrealist paintings. Modern sculptor Nikki de St Phalle also has a perfume, bottled in a flacon whose stopper is sculpted with primary-coloured serpents.

The wholesale arrival of the couturiers in the perfumery business in the 1920s changed the marketing of fragrance dramatically. As is explained more fully in the next chapter, the couturiers' perfumes had to be strongly identified with their

Above: The bottle for Salvador Dali's eponymous first commercial fragrance in 1985 was taken from his painting *L'Aphrodite de Cnide*. The bottle copies the painting exactly, down to the slant at the top of the nose.

Right: The Orient has been an enduring theme for fragrances throughout this century, especially before 1930. Bleu de Chine ('China Blue') was designed by Viard for Isabey in 1925.

style and their clothes. To many people, it would have been obvious from the start that the couturiers didn't actually compose the scent themselves. Their role was as editors, choosing the scents they thought most chic, and most appropriate for the women who wore or who aspired to wear their clothes.

Fashion designers on the whole know no more about the art of perfumery than anyone else. But what they do know about is visual style. Their dominance of fragrance since the 1920s has meant that the 'look' of perfume – its packaging, and, above all, the bottle, the most enduring part of the packaging – has become increasingly important because it can be linked to them as visual artists more surely than the scent itself. Nowadays, when we

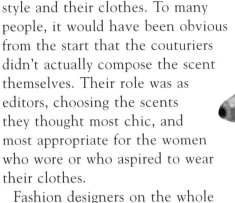

hear that a favourite fashion designer is about to launch a scent, we are as excited to know how the bottle will look as we are to know how the fragrance will smell. We assume that the designer will have had a big part to play in how the bottle looks. Sometimes, they do.

Often, the link with the clothes is made explicit. Paul Poiret, who was the first couturier to launch perfume in the 1910s, employed glass designer Schaller to create bottles which were sometimes even hand-blown at Murano in Venice. Some came swaddled in a Poiret silk handkerchief. Later it became common to have a hand-tied ribbon round a bottle's neck as though it were wearing a scarf. Sometimes bottles are designed like dresses frozen in glass. The shape of Ungaro's Diva is the glass version of one of his pleated gowns as it folds over the cleavage. Dior's Miss Dior, launched in 1947 on the same day as his famous New Look collection, was at first in an amphora-shaped

The magnificent Ming Toy was created for Forest in 1923. The name is an anglicized version of a Chinese name. Forest, a French company, often used English words, a fashionable practice at the time.

bottle in line with the tightly corseted shape of the clothes. When Dior radically changed his silhouette in 1950 to the Vertical Line, he changed the scent's outfit as well to a rectangular bottle 'cut like a tailored suit' and patterned in houndstooth tweed: the perfect symbol of the groomed, grown-up 1950s woman.

In 1921, Chanel launched a brilliant counter-attack against the bourgeois femininity and romance of perfumes with No 5. Just as her clothes appropriated items from the masculine world and made them available to women, so did her perfume. The name was borrowed from the rational, 'masculine' world of numbers, and the smell itself was classed at the time as

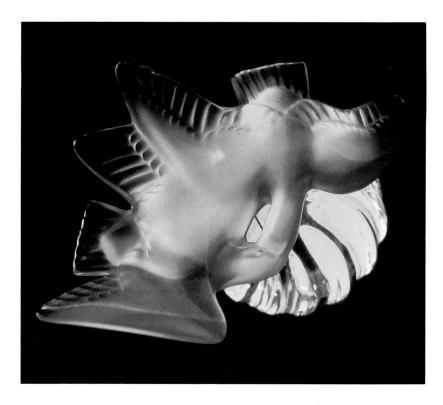

Above: Nina Ricci's L'Air du Temps of 1948 is still sold in the poetic flacon by Marc Lalique. Two doves with outstretched wings bill and coo on the stopper.

Opposite: The functional square design of Chanel No 5 has changed subtly through the twentieth century.

Left: Christian Dior's perfumes of the late 1940s and 1950s were beautifully presented, often in an amphora design by Baccarat. The bottle for Diorissimo is particularly lovely, with gilt roses and jasmine growing upwards from a crystal and gilt bottle. It is still available in a limited edition.

'androgynous' because it could not be identified as containing any particular flower or spice. And then there was the bottle: a severe, clinical square stripped of curlicues, a 'cubist' bottle that encapsulates the spirit of modernism so succinctly that it is in the Metropolitan Museum of Art in New York.

Chanel's great friend, socialite Misia Sert, claims she gave the couturier the idea of using the utilitarian bottle dispensed by pharmacies of the time. Many a pen has waxed lyrical over the drastic simplicity of this bottle and its name. If No 5 had been given a more specific look it would have dated more quickly and would sell now on its romantic evocation of an era. But that bottle is as aggressively modern now as it was then. However, it has changed subtly over the years, overhauled every decade or so in line with the current style ethos.

In 1927, a few years after Chanel's, another famous bottle appeared, the *boule noire* (black ball) of couturier Jeanne Lanvin. Designed by Armand

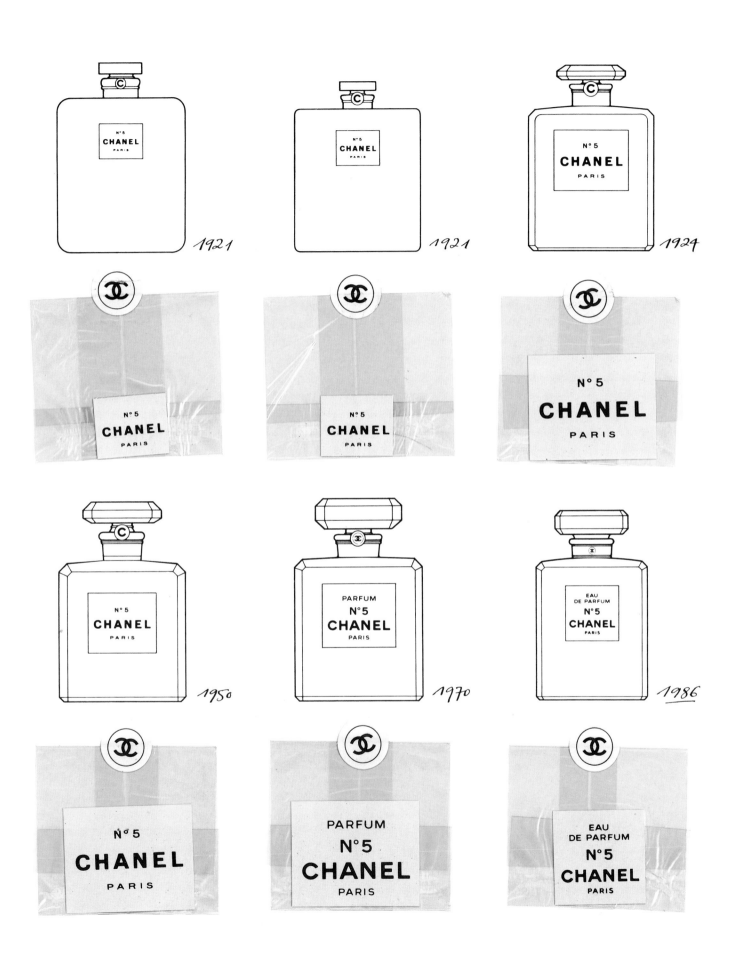

Rateau, it is stamped with an art deco logo of Lanvin and her daughter by Paul Iribe, an early example of what has become a popular theme for selling scent in the 1990s, mother love as opposed to romantic love. Limited editions in green, red and blue Sèvres porcelain were made in 1926 as presents for special clients; these have since become valuable collectors' items.

Jean Patou, the other great couturier of the 1920s, had his bottles all designed with pinecone-shaped stoppers by interior designer Louis Suë, apart from Joy, which came in a simple crystal rectangle. All were made by Baccarat. Normandie, his scent to celebrate the launching of the famous transatlantic luxury liner in 1935, is the most collectable of his flacons. In crystal, by Louis Suë for Baccarat, it has a huge aluminium model of the

The female form has been an enduring inspiration for perfume flacons from ancient times. In this century two of the most famous interpretations have been Schiaparelli's Shocking (*above*), modelled on the vital statistics of Mae West, and Jean-Paul Gaultier's eponymous perfume (*right*), whose award-winning glass flacon wears a dominatrix metal fetish-corset in the extrait version. Both make explicit reference to the couturier's art, one with a measuring tape, the other with underwear-as-outerwear, a Gaultier speciality.

Normandie sailing right through it. The special limited edition bottle with a crystal flacon tucked into the funnel of the ship was given to all first-class passengers on the ship's maiden voyage.

From the 1930s, designer Elsa Schiaparelli launched bottles quite different from Chanel's, totally of the moment, and often in collaboration with surrealist artists. Schiap, as she liked to be known, was not only Chanel's great rival, but also her opposite. As couturier Cristóbal Balenciaga rather acidly put it, 'Coco had very little taste, but it was good. Schiap, on the other hand, had lots of it and it was bad.' She invented kitsch before we had a word for it.

Schiap was not interested in good taste; she liked her fashion hot and strong and her scents the same way. The Shocking bottle of 1937 is notorious for reproducing, in miniature, the vital statistics of Mae West. West had been due in Paris for fittings with Schiap for her film *Sapphire Sal*, but she never materialized in the flesh. Instead,

Lanvin's elegant *boule noir* (black ball) appeared in 1927 with the house logo of Lanvin and her daughter.

Patou's Normandie celebrated the launch of the famous transatlantic liner in 1935.

she sent a plaster-cast of herself as the Venus de Milo and intimate details of her figure. This was the model for the costumes, but also for the bottle. It cleverly made the fashion/fragrance connection even clearer with a mini measuring tape round the dummy's neck and a bunch of coloured glass flowers where its head would have been. It was made for Schiap by the surrealist sculptress Eleonore Fini, who also gave Rochas the idea for packaging Femme.

The Shocking bottle is echoed in the recent Jean-Paul Gaultier flacon in which a torso wears a metal version of the dominatrix corset he made for Madonna's 1991 Blonde Ambition tour. The Gaultier bottle is a good example of genius marketing. The link with Madonna does as much for him as the link with Marilyn Monroe does for Chanel No 5, and by packaging it irreverently in a metal can – as he memorably put it 'like for catfood' – he sent out all the right messages to the rebellious young women who like his clothes, but usually can't afford them.

Schiaparelli's provocative Shocking was followed by an extravagant, dreamy bottle called Le Roy Soleil ('The Sun King'), designed by Salvador Dali and made by Baccarat in 1945. It was named for Louis XIV, known as the Sun King. The features of the king's face were formed from swallows, while about his face streamed the crystal rays of a watery sun, the whole resting on a blue and gilt glass sea. The bottle came in a gilded scallop shell case. As Schiap noted: 'It was too expensive and too sophisticated for the general public . . . but it was a lovely object not destined to die.' She sent one of the first bottles to the Duchess of Windsor, who wrote back: 'It really is the most beautiful bottle ever made . . . [and] has displaced the Duke's photograph on the coiffeuse!' Le Roy Soleil was launched in 1945, and soon after Schiap followed it with a saucy bottle, Zut!, which was the missing half to the Shocking torso, (just) wearing a pair of painted panties that had lost their elastic.

The period between the wars especially saw a glut of fanciful and fantastical bottles that vied with the most rococo excesses of the eighteenth century. Some were beautiful, like the amber glass Coeur de Feu ('Heart of Fire'), or the flacons in the shape of ancient oil lamps with glass flames from Mahaaga, with moulded angels kneeling to receive ambrosia from heaven in their chalices. De Marcy's Le Collier Miraculeux ('The Miraculous Necklace') of 1927 consisted of 13 graduated pearls, which, in their jewellers' box, looked exactly like a pearl necklace. In fact, all but the smallest pair were tiny flacons. Other bottles were fabulously kitsch, in the shape of jolly Buddhas, pug dogs and a light bulb for the Piver perfume Volt.

The curves of a woman's body frequently provided inspiration, especially for the couturier perfumes. Mae West crops up again as the model for Rochas' Femme ('Woman') of 1944,

Above: Between the wars, perfume bottles often revelled in out-and-out kitsch, like the famous Golliwogg series of 1919 by De Vigny. Designed by Condé Nast art director Michel de Brunhoff, the golliwog arrived in Paris as a perfume at the dawn of the Jazz Age.

Left: After the Second World War, perfume was more discreet. Femme by Marc Lalique for Rochas in 1944 set the more ladylike tone of scents to come, even though it was inspired by the curves of Mae West's hips.

first launched as a luxury limited edition. Made by Lalique, the amphora-shaped bottle apparently echoes West's woman-sized hips, and was packaged in a box covered with the black Chantilly lace of the waspie corset Rochas made for one of her film roles. This black lace has since become the signature of the house of Rochas. As often happens, it is the packaging of the perfume that ends up as the enduring symbol of a fashion house.

Originally, the box and packaging were not part of a perfume's image, but were there to protect it during transport. This began to change towards the end of the nineteenth century, but it was only with Poiret and his Rosine perfumes that the boxes became an ingenious tool for expressing the style of the fragrance. Some spectacular boxes have featured since, like the silk-lined golden scallop shell for Le Roy Soleil, as well as numerous painted cardboard cartons every bit as charming as the bottles themselves. One of the most endearing was the 1951 box for Nina Ricci's L'Air du Temps with its doves. The box was in the shape of a domed birdcage covered in pleated yellow silk and could be illuminated with an electric battery supplied in a matching pouch.

Recently, boxes have seen another leap of inventiveness with the origami-like wrapping for Kenzo's fragrances, and the tongue-in-cheek tin can for Gaultier. The modern trend for eco-friendly beauty may see packaging gradually disappear, however. The Comme des Garçons minimalist fragrance comes vacuum-packed in plastic like honey-roast ham, and Aveda's in spartan recycled board.

Bottles by Design

By the mid-1960s, fragrance had become such big business that a new profession was born, that of flacon designer. Of course, Lalique and others had designed scores of flacons early in the century, but they were glass and crystalmakers who also made a variety of other objects as well. Pierre Dinand, however, was the first to devote himself exclusively to designing perfume bottles.

Dinand specializes in bottles with a rigorous modern feel to them. One of his early bottles was Calandre for futuristic 1960s designer Paco Rabanne. Far from being a romantic evocation of flowers, Rabanne wanted his scent to be 'the representation of a couple making love in a new sports car with leather seats'. With this far-out brief, Dinand came up with a bottle modelled on the radiator grille (*calandre* in French) of a Rolls-Royce convertible, thus also giving the fragrance its name.

The Opium bottle was inspired by inro, boxes in which Japanese samurai kept opium as a painkiller for wounds.

Dinand's Obsession bottle was inspired by Calvin Klein's collections of smooth round stones and hunks of amber. Dinand combined these to make a rounded bottle with an amber cap. It has nothing to do with clothes, just the enchantment of stillness.

'Designing a bottle', says Dinand, 'is like designing a little house. The bottle is the perfume's house.' Because it will live with the designer who commissions it for years, it has to be the perfect expression of his or her concept of the fragrance. 'The bottle must be the echo chamber and materialization of their ideas,' Dinand explains.

Dinand also worked with Yves Saint Laurent on the Opium bottle of 1977. At the time the scent did not have a name. Saint Laurent and Dinand shared a love of the Orient, and Saint Laurent briefed Dinand to create a bottle that evoked the Oriental style of Napoleon III, perhaps with pompons. Dinand did not exactly follow the brief. Instead, he reworked the ornate wooden boxes called inro that Japanese samurai used to hang from their belts. These boxes were made up of several drawers held together with string passing down each side, usually with a small sculpted ball, a netsuke, in the shape of an animal on the top. The boxes held medicinal herbs, spices, salt and opium as a painkiller for when the samurai were wounded. Saint Laurent liked the design, and decided the fragrance would be called Opium, after the inro's most intriguing contents.

Dinand is known for his interest in the technical side of flaconnage, working closely with the glassmaking companies of the Bresle Valley north of Paris where 70 per cent of all fragrance bottles in the world are made. He has also produced a number of bottles using

state-of-the-art plastics – like the surlyn used for Obsession's amberlike cap – which have transformed perfume bottles in the 1980s and 1990s.

Serge Mansau, another gifted flacon designer, designs bottles with a natural rather than industrial ethos. 'When I visited his atelier, what struck me was the love of nature that was reflected in all I saw,' says designer Kenzo. This latter-day Lalique is inspired by the forms of nature for the bottles he creates, notably for Kenzo and Montana. 'Earth', he says, 'is a strange, unknown, unseen place.' It is the small-scale detritus of nature that most people automatically edit out that is his primary source of ideas: leaves, pebbles, shells, rinds, grains and ripples of sand, drops of water, the multiple forms of twigs.

Nothing is too small to be overlooked by Mansau. The inspiration for the prize-winning Montana bottle literally dropped at his feet in the helicopter shape of a winged maple seed. This was all he took to a presentation with the members of the Montana marketing department. They were expecting concept boards, maquettes and early trials in glass, when Mansau simply announced: 'This is your bottle,' and opened his hand, from which the seed slowly revolved down on to the table. The final bottle describes the seed's spiralling fall as seen by the light of a stroboscope, in sections.

When Japanese designer Kenzo first came to Mansau's studio outside Paris, he was drawn to the numerous stones there, from boulders bisected with skeins of rope (*left*), an ancient Japanese art, to tiny seaworn pebbles. To create the bottle for Kenzo's eponymous perfume (*right*), Mansau simply placed a flower on one of the stones.

Below: Mansau created the leaf bottle for Kenzo's Parfum d'Eté.

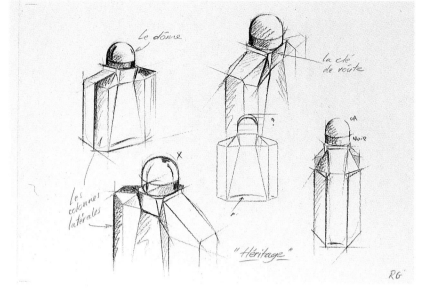

Serge Mansau's fascination with transforming unseen nature into glass and metal has led to some highly original bottles. Balahé for Léonard was conceived as a man-made stone, smooth on one side, rough and buckled on the other. Another bottle for Nino Cerruti is like a small section cut from a waterfall and frozen in frosted glass. Others, divinely expressive of the mystery of scent itself, have never seen the light of day. One enigmatic perspex stone opens to reveal a heartland of crystal, just like some real split pebbles, inside which nestles a tiny, precious flacon. The abstract nature of scent, its invisible movement round the body, inspired another series of maquettes, pairs of bottles that gyrate in the slightest breeze. Two cones sit on top of one another, each with a dimple in the base. The lower bottle balances on the fulcrum of a metal spike which sits in this dimple; its stopper rises into an identical spike on which rests the upper bottle. The slightest touch sends them rocking and spinning in a voluptuous and incredibly feminine way. The intersecting gyres make visible the way that spiralling vapour trails of perfume molecules move around the body.

To celebrate their illustrious heritage, Guerlain launched Héritage in 1992. The bottle, designed by sculptor Robert Granai, was inspired by the keystone, dome and columns of classic European architecture.

The sapphire ring (*right*) of Boucheron's eponymous fragrance, launched in 1988, was followed in 1994 by Jaipur (*below*), in the shape of an Indian Nauratan bracelet.

As Dottore Martone, President of the Accademia del Profumo in Italy, explains, 'Mansau is a genius ahead of his time. Some of his ideas are just too advanced or too expensive.' Consequently, he dreams of selling them as limited edition works of art. 'A popular fragrance is one of the most widely disseminated manufactured objects in the world,' he explains. 'If you think of the bottles as little pieces of sculpture, then these are some of the best-known sculptures in the entire

world.' Mansau has returned flacons to their ancient roots as works of art in glass, metal – and perfume.

Jeweller bottles

Jewellers occupy a special niche in twentieth-century perfumery. In the 1970s, they decided that if couturiers could form a viable link with fragrance, why, with their credentials of status and luxury, couldn't they? After all, scent bottles are accessories, like jewellery. The first to launch a fragrance was Van Cleef & Arpels with First in 1976, followed by Cartier with the ornate, status-symbol bottle for Panthère in 1986. Tiffany, Bvlgari, Chopard and Boucheron also launched scents, some more, some less linked to the idea of the jewellery. Chopard produced one called Happy Diamonds with a loose diamond clanking inside the bottle. When the perfume was finished you took the diamond to a Chopard boutique to have it set.

Perhaps the most successful of all the jeweller bottles has been the Boucheron series. It started with an eponymous fragrance in a container like a huge sapphire ring, followed by a sumptuous bath line as costly as most perfumes. The latest, Jaipur, comes in the best jeweller bottle yet, shaped like an Indian Nauratan bracelet, once given as amulets to young brides. Rajasthan legend tells that gems were formed from the fossilizing body of a demon struck down by the gods. His bones turned to diamonds, his teeth to pearls, his blood to rubies, his lymph to garnet, his nails to chrysoberyl and his fat to crystal and coral. The bracelets were originally made with nine of these stones, each of which was thought to have a particular protective power. Jaipur is also an echo of the scented, jewel-encrusted talismans people carried in Europe in previous centuries.

The pure simplicity of Issey Miyake's Eau d'Issey was designed by Fabien Baron, art director of *Harper's Bazaar* magazine. It is an icon of 1990s bottle design.

ISSEY MIYAKE

While flacon-designers like Mansau, Dinand and Joël Desgrippes produce nothing but perfume bottles, artists in other mediums continue to make significant contributions to flaconnage. Paloma Picasso, daughter of Pablo and also a jewellery designer, was inspired by a pair of her earrings for the bold circles and ellipses of her Mon Parfum. She has capitalized on the growing numbers of people who collect modern perfume bottles by producing a special limited edition design for her perfumes each year, like her Planète de Parfum of 1994.

The man who has designed the bottles most in tune with the 1990s *Zeitgeist* is graphic designer Fabien Baron, art director of *Harper's Bazaar* magazine and designer of Madonna's *Sex* book. He dreamed up the pure, architectural cone for Issey Miyake's Eau d'Issey, the 'vodka' bottle for Calvin Klein's CK1, and the prism for Lancôme's Poème.

We are at a point now where we expect the bottle to tell us something about the style of the house selling it and about the fragrance inside. The clarity and simplicity of Eau d'Issey, for example, says everything about Miyake's clothes as well as the fragrance, which Miyake wanted to smell 'pure as water'.

A plain rectangle may contain the most beautiful scent, but with all the other bottles vying to catch our eye, we are unlikely to spot it in the overstocked perfumery departments where most fragrances are bought. We have to be attracted to the look of a fragrance before we decide to investigate. As Dinand puts it: 'Touching the bottle is a woman's first contact with her fragrance.' Bottles have never been more important in selling scent than they are now.

Chapter Four

Fragrant Fashion

The first third of the twentieth century was the Golden Age of perfumery. At its beginning, perfumes were identified with the perfumers who created them. The greats were François Coty and Jacques Guerlain, but a host of other perfumers also made some wonderful scents. And then came Coco Chanel, the first couturier to really understand what's in a name. It was the six letters of hers, not the number five, that brought Chanel the sweet smell of success. She cemented a marriage between fashion and fragrance that has been one of the great commercial successes of the consumer century. Now, almost every successful fashion designer plans a fragrance as the means to financial freedom, and many designers of the past live on in little bottles of scent concocted in their name by an anonymous nose. Fragrance may be ephemeral, but in the end, it is more eternal than a dress. If, as Chanel liked to say, a woman without a perfume is a woman without a past, then a couturier without a perfume is a couturier without a future.

The Perfumers

GUERLAIN

Guerlain is a unique phenomenon in the world of perfumery. While other perfume houses have gone under or been eaten up by multinational companies, Guerlain has survived the changes of two centuries to emerge as the only perfumers who can compete with the international clout of the fashion houses. During most of this time the company remained in the family, only recently being bought by Louis Vuitton–Moët Hennessey (LVMH). Yet it has retained its character. To walk into a department store anywhere in the world and purchase a bottle of Guerlain's Samsara is to experience the cutting edge of twentieth-century perfumery. To walk into their boutique on the Champs-Elysées in Paris is to walk back in time to the charm of *belle époque* France.

The company was founded in Paris in 1828 by Pierre-François-Pascal Guerlain, son of a humble pewter-worker, who set up shop in the rue de Rivoli. At the time, anything English was hugely fashionable in Paris, and Guerlain, who had studied chemistry in England, imported English perfumes and cosmetics. Soon, however, he was experimenting with his own products, manufactured in a workshop near by.

At the 1834 Exhibition of Products of French Industry, the Guerlain stand featured an assortment of goods typical of perfumers of the day. There was *eau-de-vie de lavande rouge* for dressing cuts

Pierre-François-Pascal Guerlain, perfumer and vinegar-maker, founded the perfume dynasty in 1828 in Paris. He set up shop on the rue de Rivoli on the ground floor of the Hotel Meurice in what is now the dining-room, selling toilet waters, pomades, perfume for household linen and delicate handkerchief scents.

and burns, *vinaigrillon de Seville* for refreshing the air in your apartment, *poudre sympathique* for perfuming paper, and a *bouquet de roi* for scenting the handkerchief, plus a pomade of pure bear fat.

This first Guerlain became known for making fragrances to match a mood. The demi-monde came to him for perfumes designed to be worn for just one evening; Balzac asked him to create a scent for him to wear while writing *César Birotteau*, his novel about a perfumer. It was a world wide-awake to the seductive power of perfume, but at the same time keen to repress it. Rules of taste were dogmatic. Madame Celnart laid down the law in her *Manuel des Dames* of 1833: 'Strong odours such as musk, amber, orange blossom, tuberose and others of this kind are entirely forbidden.' She permitted only a few drops of Eau de Cologne sprinkled on a stocking or a blouse, never on to naked skin.

The ideal for a perfume of the day was not that it should be new, exciting and original, rather that it should be discreet, familiar and respectable. Guerlain made scents that conformed to the rule of taste, like Eau de Cologne Impériale, created for the Empress Eugénie in 1860, and still sold today in its original bottle studded with imperial gold bees. Eau Impériale summed up the fashion for light, fresh scents devoid of eroticism. It is a fleeting compound of lemons, oranges

and bergamot, blended with herbaceous notes of lavender and rosemary.

On Pierre-François-Pascal's death in 1864, the company passed into the hands of his two sons. One, Gabriel, took over the management, while the other, Aimé, became the nose. This dividing of the business between two brothers or cousins has been a Guerlain tradition ever since. Their father left a prosperous company, buoyed up by its association with the French royal family.

Then, as now, a famous clientele was a massive boost to such a capricious product as a perfume. Royalty and the more glamorous members of the aristocracy were like Hollywood stars. When Marilyn Monroe announced in the 1950s that she wore nothing to bed but Chanel No 5, the perfume began to sell out everywhere. Women were buying it not just for the smell, but also in the hope that it might alchemically infuse them with the allure of Monroe.

The right window in this old advertisement shows the Paris boutique, by 1840 in the rue de la Paix, while the left hand shows the factory at Colombes-sur-Seine.

An 1850 bill of sale records M. Guerlain's purchase of rose essence, vervain, citronella and cloves.

With the Empress Eugénie, it was different. Wearing a Guerlain fragrance meant you shared your refined tastes with the Empress, you were upwardly mobile. But Aimé Guerlain was not content merely to reflect the tastes of others. With Jicky in 1889, he introduced a brutally innovative bouquet that remains in a class of its own today. Jicky is a fougère or 'fern' fragrance. The fougère family already had one classic in Houbigant's Fougère Royale of 1882. The fougère note came from coumarin, a new synthetic derived from the tonka bean, which smells of new-mown hay. However, Jicky goes one step further, taking two dissonant accords and uniting them harmoniously together.

It opens with the familiar cologne freshness of citrus fruits and herbs. Lemon, lavender and bergamot are blended with mint, verbena, sweet marjoram, and the softness of coumarin. It develops into a spicy heart-note

Liù (*right*) was a typical 1930s floral bouquet based round jasmine, ylang-ylang and vanilla.

Opposite: The classic L'Heure Bleue, created in 1912 by Jacques Guerlain, was inspired by the Impressionists, whose paintings he collected. This impressionistic ad shows Paris at dusk, 'the blue hour'.

Perfume critic Luca Turin describes Jicky as opening 'with a prodigious accord which leaps four octaves from the brown of the earth to the blue of the sky. It passes by, leaving an enigmatic and smiling aura. The quintessence of the Guerlain spirit.'

that features what was another new synthetic, linalol (isolated from rosewood) interwoven with sandalwood. So far, it displays all the proper decorum. From this emerges, subtly, the aphrodisia of musk, ambergris and civet. Jicky is a fragrance which expresses both a crystalline clarity and a hidden sensuality.

It was still too shocking for Victorian women, who were expected to smell like flowers, not this enigmatic effluvia of sharpness and sensuality. Men were the first to wear it and some discerning men still wear it today, among them Sean Connery. It was only as women began to liberate themselves from sexual and economic repressions in the second decade of the twentieth century that Jicky took off. It was said when it was launched that it had been named for some belle who had captured the eye of Aimé Guerlain, but in fact Jicky was the nickname of Jacques Guerlain, Aimé's young nephew, who trained with his uncle and became the next Guerlain perfumer. Less romantic it may be, but Jicky is an apt tribute to one of the great noses of the twentieth century.

Jicky was the fragrance that began to define the Guerlain signature, the accord that is recognizable in all Guerlain perfumes since, known as the Guerlainade. Jacques Guerlain, however, was the nose that took the warmth and sophistication inherent in this accord to new heights in the first third of the twentieth century. He created

Are you her type?

LIU GUERLAIN

the masterpieces of the Guerlain stable, L'Heure Bleue, Mitsouko and Shalimar. Fragrance had moved on from the decorum of his grandfather's day to embody something more daring. The bourgeoisie still behaved according to society's rules, but they dreamed of breaking them. Perfume, once the signal of respectability, became an escape from it. A 1900 edition of the magazine *Printemps* captures the mood: 'In the heady atmosphere of the Hippique stadium, Guerlain the magician sprayed a little of his Jardin de Mon Curé, twenty drops of Tsao-Ko and a smidgeon of Jicky and suddenly, hey presto . . . we were reborn, we could breathe, we fell into an adoring ecstasy of opium perfume.' The rich, creamy notes of vanilla, musk, amber and civet were coming back into fashion, and scent was once again assuming its time-honoured role as the erotic narcotic.

Fragrances were launched then without the expensive marketing fanfare of today and consequently it hardly mattered if they lasted one year or a hundred. Jacques Guerlain was prolific, producing two or three new perfumes a year with charming names like Voilà Pourquoi J'aimais Rosine ('That's Why I Loved Rosine') and Pour Troubler ('To Perturb'), all of which have long vanished. In 1906, he composed Après l'Ondée ('After the Shower'), an evocation of hawthorn after rain, which is still sold at Guerlain in Paris and a few select stores worldwide. Then, in 1912,

96

came the classic L'Heure Bleue, named for the twilight 'blue hour' when the sense of smell gains ascendance over sight. L'Heure Bleue is a rich floral perfume, a nosegay of old-fashioned flowers on a warm bed of musk and vanilla.

Two further Guerlain classics followed in the next 13 years. First, Mitsouko in 1919, a chypre in the vein of Coty's iconoclastic Chypre of 1917, but with a brilliant peach note, made possible by a new aldehyde, C14, which another master-perfumer, Edmond Roudnitska, was to use in 1944 for Rochas's Femme. Mitsouko is a very refined perfume, a short, elegant formula, but a complex scent. As a chypre, it is based on oakmoss with elements of labdanum and patchouli. The top notes of peach and bergamot trickle down into rose, jasmine and spices.

Once again, here was a scent that reiterated the exotic nature of perfume; the name means 'mystery' in Japanese. The Orient exerted a huge fascination on the West in the first third of the twentieth century. While today we are drawn to the spiritual aspects of Eastern mysticism, the East then symbolized a languorous abandon that was miles from the repressive culture of the West. The star couturier of the period, Paul Poiret, was totally inspired by the Orient. He designed clothes that evoked the sumptuousness of Russian and Persian costume and the kimono, and held balls on the same exotic themes, like his famous 'One thousand and second night' soirée in 1911.

As Poiret himself remembers the ball, 'A half-naked African, draped in boukhara silks, carrying a torch and a scimitar, led the guests to me. They first crossed a sandy courtyard, where fountains sparkled in porcelain

The 1920s saw a vogue for the East with scents like Fille du Roi de Chine ('King of China's Daughter') and Guerlain's great classic, Shalimar.

basins . . . and found themselves in front of a huge golden cage with twirled bars in which I had locked up my "favourite mistress".' This turned out to be Madame Poiret. While a well-known actor read from the *Thousand and One Nights* and La Zambrinelhi danced, 'twenty black men and women kept myrrh and incense burners going, [and] a flute and a zither could be heard wafting from a grove and troubling the senses.'

This vision of the East, fantastical as it may be, lies at the root of a long line of fragrances known as orientals. These sweet, spicy scents are synonymous with heavy-lidded sensuality and, with an imagery to match, they are still working their old black magic in perfumes like Yves Saint Laurent's Opium and Calvin Klein's Obsession. Guerlain's most famous fragrance is an oriental, Shalimar, born in 1925, four years after Chanel No 5.

Like Jicky, Shalimar was not an instant success. Formulated in 1921, it had to wait four years to be properly launched and accepted. It is now generally held as the progenitor of all modern orientals. But Shalimar itself was a development from the oriental element in Jicky, which it pushed to new extremes. In fact, Shalimar was literally born from a fusion of Jicky and a new synthetic vanilla, vanillin ethyl. Jacques Guerlain, working in the laboratories, was delivered a phial of the new synthetic; he turned round and poured it straight into a flask of Jicky 'for no reason, just to try'. *Voilà!* The basic structure of Shalimar.

Shalimar is a name synonymous with French perfumery and an enduring

In the 1930s, many scents were inspired by the new thrill of air travel, like Vol de Nuit ('Night Flight') named for Antoine de Saint-Exupéry's novel. It is a variation on Shalimar, and still available.

success for Guerlain. The name hints at the enchantment of the Orient again; the gardens of Shalimar were created by Shah Jahan for his favourite wife, Mumtaz Mahal, in whose memory he later built the Taj Mahal. It contained 30 per cent of perfume oils, twice the amount usual at the time, and, for this reason, was initially more popular in America. It is defined by a heavy veil of vanilla, with patchouli, sandalwood, damp earthy vetiver, opopanax, amber, and the animal notes musk and civet. Good civet, much used by the Guerlains, was said to have a 'woman's' smell. Notes like these fuse with the skin, and radiate a luxurious warmth for hours.

That warmth and intimacy is also notable in Guerlain's recent success, Samsara, another oriental in which Indian jasmine is woven through a lattice of sandalwood to create a powerful characteristic aura that reverberates for many hours. If you spray on Samsara before an evening out, you will still smell it on your pillow the next day. Samsara was created in 1989, exactly a hundred years after Jicky, by the latest member of the Guerlain family to take the role of perfumer, Jean-Paul Guerlain.

Once again, the name evokes the magic of the Orient, but this time with a modern twist of mysticism. Samsara is Sanskrit for 'eternal return' and the original commercial was totally of its time. Instead of showing a flirtatious liaison, it features American model Tracy Toon wandering reverently through a Tibetan Buddhist monastery and up to a Buddha from whose hand a golden drop of Samsara falls on to her wrist. At the end of the twentieth century, with the sexual revolution almost played out, the spiritual connotations of perfume have returned to fascinate us once more.

COTY

'Perfume is a love affair with oneself,' said François Coty, ushering in the era of modern perfumery. Of all the perfumers, this Corsican is the one most widely hailed as a genius, dubbed 'the Napoleon of perfume' by envious contemporaries. Everyone copied him. They still do. Georges Vindry, the curator of the museums at Grasse, praises him as 'an ambitious visionary . . . and a true nose, with all the imagination and audacious creativity which that entails'.

Coty's genius lay in exploiting the potential of synthetics, creating fragrances that went beyond nature into an abstract realm of sophisticated new accords. In 1905 he produced L'Origan ('Oregano'), sometimes cited as the first modern perfume, a bold edifice of spices and flowers that was an immediate success and started the trend for intensely spicy florals. Opium is like L'Origan without the flowers.

But above all, it was his Chypre ('Cyprus') in 1917 which galvanized modern perfumery and gave birth not only to the chypre family of fragrances but to other scents which in their turn opened up new directions in the art. The way perfumers build fragrances even today owes much to the olfactory construction of Chypre. The fragrance seemed to float effortlessly 'as though the body of the perfume were carried on a jasmine-scented cloud', as Edmond Roudnitska has put it. It opened with stimulating top notes of bergamot, lemon, neroli and orange with a heart note of rose and jasmine and the mainly oakmoss dry-down that identifies the chypre family. Coty mastered a special blend of oakmosses that he called his 'oakmoss *bouillon*' which had more foresty coolness than

François Coty was born François Spoturno in Corsica in 1875. He moved to Paris, took the name of the mother he hardly knew, Marie Coti, and frenchified the spelling in order to give an aura of Parisian chic to his company.

Coty created Complice ('Accomplice') in 1934, but died before it could be launched. It remained on ice until 1974, when the Coty company launched it in a period design bottle.

anyone else's. Labdanum, patchouli with its peaty dampness, civet and musk also lingered in the background.

Coty's fragrances were, above all, sophisticated and urbane, bidding a permanent adieu to the pastoral floral tributes that had largely been perfumery's lot until then. In the nineteenth century the art of perfume was about fixing the notes of nature in a bottle, but just as the camera superseded painting in expressing realism, so advances in perfumery opened the way for a more impressionistic type of fragrance at the turn of the century, developing into the fully abstract 'cubism' of scents such as Chanel No 5 later on.

The chypre family of fragrances is entirely modern in mood. Scent psychologist Joachim Mensing has described chypres as 'smelling like business'. What he means is that they have none of that 'little woman' brand of femininity that sees the female sex as something akin to flower-fairies. Chypres were the fragrances of the emancipated new women who smoked, shortened their skirts and learned to drive or even fly. Throughout this century, chypres have sold well whenever women have made progress towards new economic or political independence.

A great talent as a nose was not Coty's only attribute. He also initiated modern fragrance marketing, and promoted and sold his scents internationally. One famous anecdote recounts how in 1904, in the first days of his business, a buyer at a Paris department store turned down his La Rose Jacqueminot. As Coty was leaving he 'accidentally' dropped the bottle, sending currents of this glorious rose wafting through the store. Women began to gather round, clamouring to buy it, and the store was obliged to take it on. He also understood that a fragrance must have poetry. He named his scents Vertige ('Vertigo'), Odalisque, and, swooningly, La Fougèraie au Crépuscule ('The Fern Garden at Twilight'). Chypre was sold with a rhyme on the embossed label: 'Parfum de Mousses Ambrées/ Emanant à Certaines Heures/ Des Bois et des Forêts' ('perfume of ambery mosses, emanating at certain hours from woods and forests').

Coty foresaw, too, the importance of giving a visual context to fragrance, a concept that has grown in importance as the twentieth century has developed into an almost totally visual culture. 'A perfume needs to attract the eye as much as the nose,' he said, commissioning talented flacon-designers like René Lalique and the firm of Baccarat to create images for his products. It was he who brought

L'AIMANT 'THE MAGNET' COTY

L'Aimant ('The Magnet'), launched in 1927, was one of the last fragrances produced by the house of Coty before its founder died. A magnet features in the ad (*above*) and on the label of the 1940s bottle in its whimsical glass slipper (*below*), hinting at its irresistible effect.

fine fragrance within the reach of a wide band of the middle classes, introducing the idea of perfume as affordable luxury, a concept that still drives fragrance marketing today. Many key figures in perfumery started with Coty, working at the massive factory near Paris he called Perfume City; among them the founder of Lancôme and the first head of Parfums Christian Dior.

The vast fortune that Coty made from his perfume business funded his political career and allowed him to buy *Le Figaro* and other newspapers. He died wealthy in 1934, having started life an orphan. The company was passed on to his family, who then sold it. It passed through several hands, going more and more downmarket, with the fragrances degenerating from the splendid originals to pale imitations along the way – a common fate. Happily, the Benckiser corporation bought Coty in 1992 and are in the process of bringing back some of Coty's heritage. They have relaunched a series of Coty creations, starting with Ambre Antique in 1995. The perfumes are reformulated as closely as possible to the originals by Yves Roubert and Yves de Chiris, perfumers whose grandfathers both worked with Coty. In addition, Ambre Antique is enshrined in the original exquisite Lalique design, made from a replica of the original mould which was broken after only 3,500 copies were made.

OTHER PERFUMERS

While Coty and Guerlain were weaving their magic, numerous small perfumeries in Paris and other capital cities round the world were also creating their own-brand scents and selling them to a select public from their own shops and increasingly through department stores. Among the best-known of the period are Lubin, Violet, Piver, Rigaud, Roger et Gallet and d'Orsay. Many imaginative leaps in the art were made as the market grew, and synthetics allowed for greater invention and more stable compositions. But almost all these small houses evaporated into the ether as the perfume business changed and grew from the 1920s on, and most of them have since been forgotten. A handful deserve a mention.

Begun in 1775, Houbigant is one of the oldest perfumeries still in existence. It is pre-dated only by the Farmaceutica di Santa Maria Novella in Florence (1612) and by Floris, the English perfume company that began in 1730 (see Chapter One). Houbigant appeared in Paris in 1775 as 'glovers and perfumers' and was soon supplying Marie-Antoinette and the royal court. By 1880, it was partly owned by Paul Parquet, a distinguished perfumer and the first to utilize synthetics in his Fougère Royale of 1882.

Another perfumer, Robert Bienaimé, joined the company at the turn of the century and went on to create in 1912 the deceptively simple masterpiece that earned him the title of one of the century's great perfumers, the classic light floral Quelques Fleurs ('A Few Flowers'). Flower fragrances, of course, were nothing new, but the majority had either sought to reproduce

Caron's En Avion of 1930 reflected the decade's vogue for air travel, almost as glamorous then as the idea of space travel is now.

Millot's famous Crêpe de Chine of 1925 was one of the world's most successful perfumes in the 1920s. This advertisement describes Crêpe de Chine as 'The perfume that envelops you like silk.'

a single flower – rose, orange blossom, sweet pea – or else were mingled with a variety of non-floral ingredients. In Quelques Fleurs, however, the world had what is often described as the first floral bouquet. It has airy topnotes of crushed leaves which quickly develop into limpid flower essences: rose, lilac, violet and jasmine, among others. It is still sold by Houbigant today.

Parfums Caron were, by contrast, brand new in 1904, established by young perfumer Ernest Daltroff. He bought the name for his company from a small shop typical of the time, which sold ribbons, scarves and scents mixed up crudely to customers' specifications in the back of the shop. Like Coty, Daltroff quickly realized the importance of marketing his fragrances internationally, and his Narcisse Noir ('Black Narcissus') of 1911 was a success around the world, especially in America. It is warm and elegant, composed of orange blossom and bergamot with woody and earthy undertones. Poivre ('Pepper') from Caron has a pungent aroma of cracked peppercorns wrapped in spicy carnations. Launched alongside in 1954 was a lighter version with a more audacious name: Coup de Fouet ('Crack of the Whip'). Women's lib, after all, was just around the corner, and Caron had always catered to liberated women.

Caron's great original, though, was its Tabac Blond ('Blonde Tobacco') of 1919, a true flapper's fragrance. At the time, smoking cigarettes was risqué and highly fashionable for women. Tabac Blond was created for the siren smoker. It's the kind of scent you can imagine Marlene Dietrich wearing. The top note is mainly orange blossom, the heart notes classic flowers, but the base note is tobacco, accented with leather, benzoin, civet, moss and cedarwood. The daring tobacco note makes Tabac Blond unique among women's fragrances. It is still available together with other Caron fragrances in a few department stores worldwide and at their small boutique on the Avenue

POIVRE
NOUVEAU PARFUM A SUCCES DE CARO

Poivre ('Pepper') from Caron had a wonderful aroma of pepper – the bottle was studded with peppercorns.

Caron's Tabac Blond ('Blonde Tobacco') of 1919 was tinged with tobacco and aimed at the daring new flappers who smoked. This flapper is wearing Poiret.

Montaigne in Paris, where the scents are decanted for customers from Baccarat crystal urns.

Molinard, venerable Grasseois perfumers, also made their mark in the first third of the century. Established in 1849, the company is still owned by descendants of the family who sell their scents from their museum in Grasse and in a few boutiques. In 1921, they launched their famous Habanita in its Lalique flacon, a sultry, enveloping oriental scent softened by a few simple flowers.

Millot was once a famous name in perfumery. Established in the nineteenth century, it produced many fine fragrances, but the most famous was Crêpe de Chine in 1925, which perfectly captured the powdery, fugitive smell of scented silk. This great classic and international bestseller was created by Jean Desprez, the great-grandson of the original Millot's wife. He later went on to launch a perfume business in his own name. Many people have assumed Desprez to be an obscure French couturier, but it was, in fact, the name of this gifted perfumer who went on to concoct the enduring classic Bal à Versailles in 1962, a vestige of the days when perfumers ruled the world of fragrance.

The rule of the perfumers was broken in 1921 when Coco Chanel launched the revolutionary Chanel No 5. In every way, Chanel No 5 is the scent of the twentieth century. Of course, it was not concocted by Chanel. Her contribution was the branding of her name and the selling-power of her cachet. It was at this point that selling a perfume began to have nothing to do with the identity of its creator and everything to do with the identity of those potent disseminators of style, fashion designers.

The Couturier-perfumers

POIRET

Chanel was not the first couturier to think of perfume. That honour belongs to Paul Poiret, the first modern fashion designer, who swept out the trappings – and corsets – of the nineteenth century and inaugurated the twentieth when he shortened women's skirts. Poiret was a great innovator, but, unlike Chanel, not a great businessman. Where she was practical, he was a dreamer. Always identifying himself with the artists of his era, his definition of an artist was someone who puts himself into everything he does. And Poiret did everything as well as design clothes: painting, writing and designing theatrical sets and interiors. Always intrigued by the mysterious attraction and symbolism of perfume, in 1911 he launched a full-blooded perfumery business with laboratory, glass-factory and packaging facilities to embody his heady visions of what scent could be.

Whereas in the 1920s, couturiers rapidly caught on to the idea that perfume equals profit plus excellent publicity, Poiret's perfumes, like his parties, were opulent phantasms of his imagination. He enshrined his scents, designed to reflect the spirit of his dresses, in glorious but expensive flacons, some of handblown glass, and adorned them with names that reeked of ancient myth and mystery – Le Bosquet d'Apollon ('Apollo's Grove'),

Poiret was the first couturier to launch perfumes. His bottles reflected the opulence and fantasy of his clothes (*opposite, left*). From then on, fashion and fragrance were made for each other.

Antinéa où Au Fond de la Mer ('At the Bottom of the Sea'), Aladin, Borgia, Le Fruit Défendu ('Forbidden Fruit') – or of whimsy – Le Mouchoir de Rosine ('Rosine's Handkerchief'), Le Parfum de Ma Marraine ('My Godmother's Perfume'). Since he was known as 'the pasha of Paris', it was appropriate that the majority had an oriental tendency. They were mostly composed by Almeras, who later created Joy for Jean Patou.

Poiret's fate could have been very different if he had seen the potential in disseminating the Poiret name to a wider clientele through his perfumes. But instead of branding them 'Poiret', he named the company Les Parfums de Rosine, after one of his daughters. Hard to imagine Donna Karan, for example, doing that now. It was a huge marketing opportunity lost. On the other hand, Poiret was acute in other ways. He employed artists like Paul Iribe, Raoul Dufy and Georges Lepape to collaborate on the perfume's image. And he understood the media. He was the first couturier to become a celebrity, and persuaded famous actresses of the day to endorse his scents. One of them, Mlle Spinelly, was photographed 'biting' into a 'forbidden fruit' painted on her salon wall. Poiret also convinced his couture clients that fragrance was the natural corollary of fashion. 'That dress fits you wonderfully,' he told them, 'but put one drop of my perfume

on its hem, and the dress will make you ravishing.'

Poiret also perfected the idea of fine packaging that further evokes the mood of the fragrance. One of his ventures was to found an art school named for his other daughter, Martine, and also a workshop named for his son, Colin. It was the designers at Atelier Colin who made some of the packaging, and the students at Martine who often painted the Rosine perfume bottles and packaging to reflect the name. Le Balcon came in a bottle with its own curlicued balcony; Le Minaret was embalmed in a tower; Borgia had a coiling serpent motif, and Le Fruit Défendu, presaging Dior's Poison, came in an apple flacon.

The changes wrought by the First World War saw Poiret's star decline. He went off to fight in the war, leaving behind couturiers either female or too old to fight to further their careers. His only creation during the war was Sang de France ('Blood of France'), a scarlet-tinted perfume that came in a heart-shaped bottle. Poiret sold the rights of his couture business to his backers in 1925 and the Rosine company was liquidated in 1929. He died in obscurity in 1944.

Aladin, *above*, was one of Poiret's many fanciful creations. The unusual metal bottle modelled on an ancient perfume-burner with its chain came in a box printed with a Persian miniature, while Le Fruit Défendu (*below*), in the shape of a stylized apple, came in a silver box covered with jungle foliage.

CHANEL

For ten years, Poiret was the only couturier to associate perfume with fashion. Then, in swift succession, came Chanel, Worth, Lanvin, Patou and a host of others, all eager to explain that, as the final invisible emanation of style, perfume had to harmonize with the clothes. In one way, this was pure hype, and many a 'designer fragrance' since has been about little more than the smell of money. But in other ways, it made perfect sense. In the centuries prior to the abstemious nineteenth, scent was integral to clothes, enclosed as it was in pearl-encrusted chatelaines and pomanders that decorated the body even as they perfumed it.

But more importantly, how as an aspect of taste could perfume, and eventually the whole beauty industry, resist being sucked in to the sphere of the fashion designer, whose cult has been so powerful this century? Fashion designers give fragrance a look, they turn it into a highly concentrated style bulletin that expresses the same concept of chic as their clothes. We are vague and uneducated about the olfactory world, but we are acute visual interpreters. If perfume was ever going to be a big part of modern culture, it was going to have to dissociate itself somewhat from the obscure world of smell and latch on to the visual arts.

Some perfumers resented the abrupt insurrection of the couturiers into their territory. 'In the eyes of these professionals, the couturier is no more gifted in making perfumes than the perfumer in making dresses,' explained one French newspaper, *l'Excelsior*, in 1927. The French writer Colette gave the fashion designers a spirited defence

This early ad (*above*), drawn by the cartoonist Sem, a friend of Chanel, showed her streamlined clothes alongside the bottle. In fact, some sources claim that Sem designed the bottle, with its masculine brutalism.

'Fashion fades, only style remains,' Chanel once said. She herself had fantastic style, as can be seen in this Horst portrait of the 1930s (*opposite*). Like her style, her most famous fragrance, No 5, has transcended fashion to become the scent of the century.

in her *L'Opèra de l'Odorat*, a paean to her friend, couturier Jeanne Lanvin. She began with an attack on pre-1920s scents that might ring a bell for those who hated the carpet-bombing perfumes of the 1980s: 'An ephemeral brutality, a legacy of the First World War, made women bathe themselves in fragrances that seemed to invoke the dreadful spirit of a savage pharmacopoeia, in dreadful perfumes which I liked to call 'Cudgel Blow', 'Ox Killer' or 'Violence' . . . in restaurants they killed my appetite, at the theatre they put me off the play.'

Colette saw the couturiers as saviours, aware that their influence could only boost French perfumery around the world: 'The couturier knows better than anyone what women need. . . . In their hands, perfume becomes a complement to getting dressed, an imponderable and necessary panache, the most indispensable of superfluities. Thanks to the couturier-perfumer, perfume can become more than a mere note in the orchestration of elegance: it can, it must represent the melodic theme, the clarity, the direct expression of the tendencies and tastes of our epoch.'

Chanel No 5 cemented this highly successful fusion between scent and sight. Nothing so perfectly expresses the modernism of Chanel as that stark little bottle and its enigmatic cargo of chic. French writer Paul Morand called Chanel 'the exterminating angel of the twentieth century'. Luxury for us is minimalism. Chanel made this true, in her way, as much as Le Corbusier.

A perfume today is nothing without a story, and Chanel No 5 tells many. The *über* story runs like this. In 1921, Chanel asked an unknown young

Ernest Beaux, creator of Chanel No 5, in his laboratory. He described his noble creation as 'the smell of a snowy landscape'.

perfumer, Ernest Beaux, to compose a perfume unlike anyone else's for her couture house. 'A woman', she is supposed to have said, 'should not smell of roses.' In due course, Beaux returned with five samples. Chanel, lying on the sofa with a terrible headache, dismissed him with a wave of her handkerchief, telling him to leave them on the mantelpiece, she would examine them later. No sooner had Beaux left, however, than she struggled from the sofa and quivered her nostrils over each in turn. When Beaux returned, it was all decided. Chanel announced: 'It's number five,' in one fell swoop allotting and naming her talisman.

This story may be true, but it also has all the markings of a modern myth:

the cabbalistic mystery of numbers; the shadowy messenger Beaux whisking in with five nameless bottles, only one of which disguises the magic potion; the fact that Chanel has a headache. Like blind Homer or deaf Beethoven, the senses-impairing headache is a sign that this was no ordinary choice – it was psychic, inspired. Chanel, whose standing as a prophetess of taste is huge, chose No 5 the way a blind seer instinctively sees the real truth because his everyday sight is dead.

Did Beaux really deliver five little flacons? The Chanel archives indicate that in fact he delivered two batches of samples, numbered 1 to 5 and 20 to 24. If this is correct, then the two batches were probably two perfumes, each offered in a few slight variations, which is common perfumer's practice. According to this version of history, Chanel launched No 22 first, then chose No 5 to appear at her *couture defilé* a few months later on 5 May. No 5 was not, then, Chanel's first, inspired choice. What is certain, though, is that five was Chanel's lucky number. It all goes back to the number five patterned on the floor of a corridor in the orphanage where she spent seven years of her childhood. How could she not have chosen number five for her signature fragrance, even if it had smelt of stinkweed? This element of Fate feeds the legend even more.

But of course it did not smell of stinkweed, it smelt of nothing else in the world. Beaux had created an audacious liquid that was the perfect expression of *luxe, calme et volupté*. The suaveness of No 5 comes from the most noble oils – an extravagant proportion of jasmine with *rose de mai*, orris root, and neroli blended with vanilla, woody and animal base notes. But the genius is that it smells not a bit like any of them, thanks to the alchemy of aldehyde crystals in a huge proportion. Some aldehydes had already been used discreetly in perfumery, but they were hard to stabilize. Beaux managed to fix them, splashing a mammoth dose into his refined bouquet. But did he mean to? According to English perfumer Arthur Burnham, who met Beaux, the answer is no. He says Beaux was quite happy to admit that it was an accident, which occurred because his new assistant did not add the usual aldehyde mixture, diluted at 1 part to 10 of alcohol, to that fifth bottle. Instead, he sloshed in the undiluted aldehyde, ten times stronger. Beaux rushed the bottles to Chanel without checking them, and she chose the fifth. When Beaux got the bottle back to the laboratory, he nearly fainted with

A Sem cartoon shows Chanel overseeing the fitting of a couture gown in the 1920s, inside a bottle of No 5, which Sem gently satirized as 'Cocologne'.

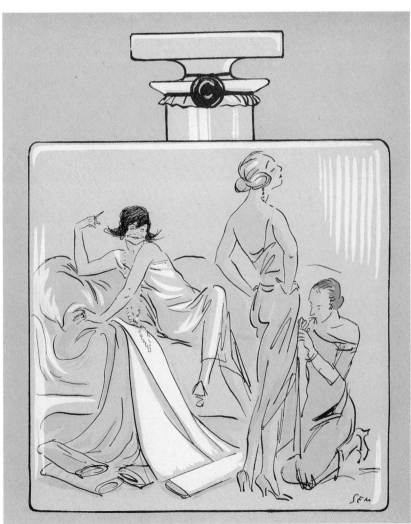

astonishment at the smell. But of course, he said nothing.

Fateful accident or not, Chanel No 5 is a masterpiece. Even though aldehydes have become the hallmark of French perfumery, no scent has ever harnessed them with such finesse. Their effect is to increase the fragrance's diffusion and give it sparkle. But more importantly, aldehydes transposed the fragrance into something completely original, something that smelt like nothing in nature, but richer, more seductively resonant, always tantalizingly on the edge of becoming a recognized aroma, but always escaping. Chanel No 5 is the most mysterious, and therefore the most desirable, of all fragrances.

That warmth and effusiveness of aldehydes, causing the scent to spring out of the bottle and spiral round the body, is something we take for granted now. But back then, scents were not so stable. If you wanted to remain scented all evening, you had to douse yourself with an inordinate amount of perfume, meaning that your fragrance started out strident in order to remain detectable. These were the scents that Colette derided as 'ox-killers'. Chanel No 5 put an end to that.

No 5 has always been linked with Russia. Paris in the 1920s underwent 'Russianization' with the influx of many thousands of White Russian émigrés, who arrived at a time when their country was already highly fashionable in the French capital, thanks to the Russian Ballet and to the orientalist vogue. Chanel's lover at the time was an émigré, Grand Duke Dmitri. No court in Europe had ever equalled the passion for perfume of the Russian court, and it has often been suggested that it was Dmitri who introduced her to another émigré, Ernest Beaux. Beaux's father had been perfumer to the tsars, and he too had worked as a perfumer in Russia. Chanel was not a fragrance-lover in her early days; she had always suspected perfumed women of having 'bad smells to hide'. Perhaps Dmitri persuaded her otherwise.

Beaux, the alchemist in the story, once memorably described his creation as smelling of 'a snowy landscape'. The Chanel archive is even more poetic about this wintry theme: 'In 1920, during the war when [Beaux] fought in the White Army, he discovered the midnight sun not far from the Pole. The lakes there gave forth an unknown scent. He kept this memory close to his heart, and the emotion it inspired would pursue him for many years to come. This is what he re-created when he concocted No 5.'

Beaux had worked for the Rallet Perfumery in Russia from 1889 to 1914 but, according to the perfumer and writer Edmond Roudnitska, was not fighting the Communists in 1920 but comfortably settled at La Bocca near Cannes. Roudnitska's short history of No 5 then takes a very prosaic turn. He insists that Beaux had created a perfume for Rallet known as Rallet No 1, which had been a flop in Russia. Rallet offered it to Chanel (who changed its number to 5) and supplied the fragrance during its early years. No 5 did not do well at first. It was only when the powerful Wertheimer Group, which owned Parfums Bourjois, took over the business of producing and marketing it in 1924 that it began to gain acclaim. Beaux became the technical director of Parfums Chanel and went on to create a handful of other very lovely fragrances – Bois des Iles ('Wood of the Isles'), Gardénia and the splendid Cuir de Russie ('Russian Leather') – which are still available today from Chanel boutiques.

If Beaux came up with the scent of No 5, and Chanel gave it chic, Marilyn Monroe added sex. Stepping off a plane in Japan in the 1950s, she was asked what she wore in bed. 'The only thing I wear to bed is a little Chanel No 5,' she replied. In fact, she was just repeating an old advertising slogan from the 1930s. Sales of No 5 shot up worldwide, and have stayed there ever since.

The intrigue surrounding No 5 does not end even there. Edmonde Charles-Roux, Chanel's biographer, and others suggest quite different machinations at work in the birth of the scent. According to this version, Beaux went to work for Coty on returning from Russia. While there, he perfected the scent that is No 5, but, due to its cost, Coty hesitated to launch it. Frustrated, Beaux departed for La Bocca with his formula which he then presented, in a few variations, to Chanel more or less in line with the legend. We will never know if this version is true. As Charles-Roux puts it: 'Who was this [chemist] who went over to the enemy?

Did he leave on his own initiative or was he bought? Was his name Ernest Beaux? All questions being met by the impenetrable silence of those who know, we must be content to leave this point in darkness.' What is certain is that in 1927 Coty launched a perfume that was almost identical to No 5, L'Aimant. The plot, or perhaps we should say the 'jus', thickens . . .

Chanel's fortune, reported as US $15 million at the time of her death in 1971, was owed to this one little perfume, shrouded in conflicting stories. It propped up the fluctuating fortunes of her couture business as perfume has done for numerous other fashion houses ever since. By 1929, it was already billed as 'The Largest-selling Perfume in the World'. Chanel's story is the blueprint of many other couturier-perfumer's, not least in terms of the tensions between herself and the Wertheimers, who produced and sold No 5. She spent years fighting to have 'her' perfume back, while they wanted to protect a lucrative business that in all fairness they had nurtured with skill.

Chanel was nothing if not a trooper. She hassled them nimbly, sneaking new perfumes on to the market which they ordered withdrawn, smuggling samples into the States which they had confiscated by customs officials, even threatening to launch a new, improved No 5 that would put paid to the old one. The 'perfume wars' of recent years have been tame compared to the steely skirmishings of Chanel. Like many designers since, she saw selling her name to another company as the equivalent of selling her soul to the devil. Once done, forever regretted – even if the other company marketed it better than she could.

In the end, she won the battle handsomely. In 1947, in addition to her other returns, Pierre Wertheimer

Chic to the end, Chanel walked each day across the rue Cambon from her suite at the Ritz to her boutique at No 31. This picture was taken in 1962; she died nine years later in 1971.

consented to pay Coco a 2 per cent royalty on the gross sales of her perfumes all over the world (about US $1 million a year). To celebrate, she took ten years off her age and became 55. Not for nothing did couturier Balenciaga say: 'Chanel is an eternal bomb. None of us can defuse her.'

FROM LANVIN TO SAINT LAURENT

Hardly had the ink dried on the first bottle of No 5 before the bandwagon was rolling and the other couturiers were launching scents right, left and centre. Jean-Philippe Worth, son of the famous couturier, had had the idea of offering his clients perfumes at about the same time as Chanel. In 1922, Worth launched Dans la Nuit in its Lalique frosted blue bottle sprinkled with stars. This was followed by, among others, Je Reviens in 1932, which is still sold. The name has an amorous history, derived from a letter Napoleon sent to Josephine from his Italian campaign: 'Je reviens en trois jours, ne te laves pas' ('I return in three days: don't wash yourself').

Molyneux knew no shame when he launched his own Numéro Cinq in 1925 (his excuse: his couture house was at No 5, rue Royale). Hot on his heels were Jeanne Lanvin and Jean Patou, both of whom commissioned talented perfumers, glass-designers and artists to create and advertise their signature scents.

Lanvin had a number of scents made up by a Russian, Madame Zed, in the early 1920s, but they were not commercialized. Instead, they were offered only to clients of the couture, a common practice at the time. In 1924 she hired a very young perfumer, André Fraysse, to be house perfumer. After My Sin in 1925, he went on to create for her what Roudnitska has called 'the most spectacular tetralogy in the history of perfumery': Arpège (1927), Scandal (1931), Rumeur (1932) and Prétexte (1937). Judging as a fellow-perfumer, Roudnitska's own particular

Jeanne Lanvin, the daughter of concierges, opened her fashion house in 1890. It is now the oldest in Paris.

Lalique designed this midnight blue, starry globe for Worth's Dans la Nuit.

love was Scandal, which he described to me once as 'a ravishing flower snapped into a fine leather handbag'. Beaux, too, had complimented its 'exquisite tastefulness'. It made use of that disturbingly erotic leather note too underused in feminine perfumery.

Of the four, only Arpège remains, French for the musical term 'arpeggio', a name given to it by Lanvin's musician daughter, the Comtesse de Polignac. It is generally considered one of the finest products of perfume's golden age, an aldehydic, spicy floral with cool, dark undertones of vetiver and patchouli. Its layered sophistication defines it as what the French call a *'parfum fourrure'* or a perfume which goes well with the animal luxury of furs. After Lanvin's death, as often happens, the fragrance and packaging were gradually altered and it bore only passing resemblance to the original. In 1993, however, L'Oréal, which now owns Parfums Lanvin, returned to the old formulation and the famous art deco ball-shaped black bottle.

Patou

Long before Calvin Klein's CK1, in 1929 Jean Patou launched a unisex perfume, Le Sien ('His/Hers'), linking it explicitly with current directions in fashion. 'With sports clothes being sober and practical,' he explained, 'a very feminine perfume would strike a false note. Le Sien is a perfume with a more masculine note. I have created this healthy, fresh, outdoors mood, a perfume which suits men, but which also goes very well with the personality of the modern woman, who plays golf, smokes, and drives her motorcar

at 120 kilometres an hour.' Of course, he had not actually created it, but the marketing-speak that makes perfumers disappear was already in place.

Patou brought to fragrance some of the insouciant humour of the period the French call '*les années folles*' (the crazy years). His first perfumes in 1925 were a trio designed to match blondes, brunettes or redheads. Next, he installed a cocktail cabinet downstairs at his couture house in the rue Saint Florentin, complete with a waiter. Cocktails were a new craze at the time, but this one allowed you to mix up perfumes instead of drinks from bottles marked 'Angostura', 'Dry' and 'Bittersweet'. Later, he played on the

Lanvin began by making clothes for her daughter, Marie-Blanche, and then commercially for children. By 1909 she was also making youthful, breezy clothes for their mothers.

The Lanvin logo, designed by Paul Iribe, captured the mother-and-daughter theme of the house. But while mother-love was sweet, in the 1920s sin was in and the names of the Lanvin scents in this ad reflect that.

As one of the first couturier-perfumers, Jean Patou knew the importance of linking perfume to his dress designs. 'Perfume is one of the most important accessories of a woman's dress,' he told American newspapers in 1927.

Patou made many pronouncements persuading women that he knew best when it came to fragrance as well as fashion: 'A refined woman . . . must perfume herself with the same discretion, taste and distinction that she displays in her clothes.' In other words, leave it to him.

flapper's rebellious penchant for smoking when he designed bottles shaped like lighters.

Joy, second only to Chanel No 5 in worldwide fame, appeared in 1930. Patou had taken on the doyenne of café society, Elsa Maxwell, to be his publicity agent. Together, they went to Grasse to see perfumer Henri Almeras. He offered them one phial after another to smell, but nothing was right. Finally, in frustration, Almeras indicated that he had one last sample, a blend based on rose de mai and jasmine de Grasse, but added 'There's no point considering that one, it's too expensive to market.' Perhaps he knew the effect this would have. At any rate, Patou and Maxwell swooped on the bottle, cried 'Eureka!' in unison, and bought it, grandly dismissing the idea that it could be diluted to make it cheaper. One of perfume's most enduring ad-lines – 'the costliest perfume in the world' – was penned almost immediately by Maxwell, based on the incident. This idea of the world's costliest perfume is as closely linked with Joy as the thought of

Marilyn Monroe naked in bed is with Chanel No 5.

Joy was first formulated in 1926, but was made available only to Patou's couture clients. Launching it on the international market in 1930 may have been a strategy to combat the drastic drop in couture sales as a result of the Crash of 1929. Over a thousand perfumes were launched in France between 1920 and 1935, but the Crash killed off or fatally weakened numerous small independent perfumers, while the couturier-perfumers, thanks to the diversification of their products and the way publicity for their clothes also boosted perfume sales, survived. The economic changes that came after the

Second World War weeded out most of the rest of the small old-fashioned perfumers proper, at the same time as a second wave of couturier-perfumers came to the fore with a host of new perfumes that had their finger on the fashionable pulse. By 1955, couturier-perfumers were the norm and perfumers were an anomaly. Only Guerlain survived intact.

The couturiers who did well with fragrance harnessed the skills of the handful of wholesale fragrance and flavour companies like Roure Bertrand. Louis Amic of Roure Bertrand, in return, cleverly cultivated the custom of the couturiers. These manufacturers, most of which began as chemical companies, constantly moved the goalposts by creating new and better synthetics and fine-tuning the analysis of natural oils. By the 1950s, companies like Firmenich had competely changed the perfume game. They could buy natural products in bulk, getting better prices, they could offer weird and wonderful new synthetics that took heavily funded research facilities to develop, and their phalanx of perfumers could cater to clients' different tastes.

The couturiers had other advantages over the perfumers. Many moved in artistic circles and commissioned avant-garde bottles, packaging and illustrations that gave their presentation an edge. The story of scent this century has been about the increasing importance of image. Poiret had asked Iribe and Lepape to work for him, the omnipresent Christian (Bebe) Bérard worked for Paquin and Elsa Schiaparelli, Cassandre the painter for Lucien Lelong, Fernand Léger for furriers Revillon, Sem for Chanel. The list is long. But the couturier who is most closely associated with artists is Schiaparelli.

Couturier perfumes sell on their association with the most élite and expensive fashions. Joy became the favourite perfume of the rich. Chanel was not a fan of this rival to No 5: 'Joy', she remarked, 'is something for prudish women who want to put their petty morals on display.'

Schiaparelli

Elsa Schiaparelli was drawn to the spirit of the Surrealists. She collaborated with several artists like Jean Cocteau and Man Ray and the poet Aragon, who designed her a necklace like a string of aspirins, but most famously with Salvador Dali, with whom she designed a surreal hat in the shape of a shoe and printed a 1.5 m (5 ft) scarlet lobster down one evening dress. He also designed the bottles for her sumptuous Roy Soleil ('Sun King') and Sleeping, which came in the shape of a candle in a little candlestick for carrying up to bed. Her most famous fragrance, still available today, is Shocking, in its shocking pink box and hourglass bottle scaled down from the vital statistics of Mae West (see Chapter Three). Shocking was a flagrantly sexy offering among the regulation rows of smart rectangular bottles. Looking like a little fertility fetish, it is stuffed full of aphrodisiac ingredients, and, at the time, was rumoured to have been based on the *odorata sexualis* of a woman.

In her autobiography, *Shocking Life*, Schiaparelli writes about the bottle and its presentation. Her first disappointment in life had been her own first name, Elsa. She referred to herself as Schiap instead. Like Chanel, she was superstitious. 'The name had to begin with an S, this being one of my superstitions,' she wrote. The idea for the name came from the bright pink colour she chose for the packaging. 'The colour flashed in front of my eyes. Bright, impossible, impudent, becoming, life-giving . . . a colour of China and Peru but not of the West – a shocking colour, pure and undiluted. So I called the perfume "Shocking".' Thus Schiap christened not only a new perfume but a new colour. 'The presentation would be shocking and most of the accessories and gowns would be shocking [that season].' What better send-off for a shocking new scent than that it be launched at a shocking pink fashion show?

But Schiap went one better; Dali was called in. He dyed a huge stuffed bear in shocking pink and gave it a bellyful of drawers. It appeared in the boutique,

Elsa Schiaparelli, doyenne of surrealist fashion.

The connection between fashion and fragrance is always present in the advertisements for Shocking – although these were usually as startling as the bottle and fragrance itself.

dressed in an orchid satin coat and hung about with jewellery. Scent-sprayers assiduously puffed Shocking all around the boutique to intrigue anyone who entered. Bebe Bérard took to dousing his beard in it 'till it trickled on his torn shirt and the little dog in his arms'. Marie-Louise Bousquet, a famous hostess and socialite 'would pull up her skirts and drench her petticoats with it'. What Shocking smelt like (sweet and piquant) was in a way irrelevant. It was talked about until it became an irresistible accessory to a fashionable life, but a very different sort of fashionable life to that of the tasteful bourgeoise who wore Chanel suits and No 5. Irish novelist Derry Quinn captured the difference in *The Fear of God*: 'He thought, in about 30 seconds she'll get up and leave the room. A few minutes later, she'll come back wearing a chiffon negligé and smelling faintly of Chanel No 5. In about 30 seconds she left the room. She came back a few minutes later, naked and wearing Shocking. He was on his feet.'

By a strange twist of fate it is often their scent that stands for a designer's style more than any of the clothes they design. Fashion is an art driven by change. Scent is the opposite. The aim, when launching a fragrance, is to create a classic that will go on for years. If this happens, it becomes the symbol of the fashion house. While clothes express the constantly evolving *Zeitgeist* of a couturier, the scent is the hieroglyphic that we have come to believe encapsulates the very essence of his or her style.

Rochas and Givenchy

By 1945, the connection between fashion and fragrance was so established that couturier Marcel Rochas held an exhibition on the theme to mark the launch of his perfume, Femme ('Woman') in 1945. 'Les Parfums à Travers la Mode 1765–1945' gave a stamp of historical authenticity to his venture. Here again, Mae West played her part. Rochas had designed costumes for her in various film roles, and the rounded bottle was supposedly modelled on her ample hips. The fragrance was soon a classic, formulated by a nose who was to become famous, Edmond Roudnitska.

Rochas found Roudnitska working in Grasse in 1943. It was wartime and the luxurious natural ingredients that went into fragrances were scarce – and so

Hubert de Givenchy was as elegant and well-bred as the clothes he designed from 1952 to 1995, most famously for Audrey Hepburn.

Below: Couturier Marcel Rochas designed costumes for Mae West, seen here in an outfit with the Chantilly lace that became his signature. The bottle of Femme is modelled on West's curvaceous hips.

were luxury foods. Perfumers had to diversify. At the time, Roudnitska was experimenting with a butter substitute in gel form that came from the same base as soap, 'fantastic in pâtisserie'. Rochas came looking for a perfume and Roudnitska gave him the only one he had, a sweet but grown-up chypre packed with white flowers, and with a distinctive peach top note. Rochas gave it that perfect name and a classic was born. Femme was the fragrance that dominated the 1950s and gave rise to a long series of chypres throughout the decade. It was Rochas's wedding present to his third wife, the famously beautiful Hélène.

Many other couturiers launched important new scents in the 1940s and 1950s. Hubert de Givenchy, the couturier who dressed Audrey Hepburn for the films *Funny Face* and *Breakfast at Tiffany's* (and ever after) was also a shrewd businessman. In 1957 he launched L'Interdit, a fragrance which could be described as the 'daughter' of

118

No 5. Audrey Hepburn, who always wore Givenchy, starred as the 'face' of the fragrance. Many wonderful 1940s and 1950s fragrances, like Jacques Fath's Iris Gris ('Grey Iris'), have been tragically discontinued, victims of a commercial attitude that cares little for the women who loved their old fragrances like best friends. But Madame Grès's Cabochard of 1959 can still be found, a leather chypre of great elegance, summing up the fashion of the 1950s for tailored, powdery fragrances that were the olfactory equivalent of the era's slickly groomed clothes. Grès's story is a cautionary one for fashion designers. She sold the rights to her scent to Beecham's and, without any royalties to support her, died in penury.

A happier story is that of couturier Nina Ricci, whose L'Air du Temps ('The Spirit of the Times') has become one of the best-selling perfumes in the world. Launched in 1948, with a dove stopper symbolizing the recent peace, its tender sweetness and romantic bottle perfectly mirrored the spirit of the New Look which was changing fashion and it was soon selling up a storm, and still is. Luca Turin describes it and its stablemates with some humour in her perfume guide: 'The feminine perfumes of Nina Ricci resemble Mills & Boon heroines . . . on page 67 they kiss the great surgeon for the first time, on page 231 the sun goes down on the *faraglioni* of Capri, in short, happy ever after.' She adds, of course, that it is very beautiful.

Robert Piguet's Fracas was yet another great perfume of the era. This can still be hunted down in both Europe and America. The name Piguet is long-forgotten as a fashion designer but his Fracas lives on and has even gained a cult following today, especially among the socialites of New York.

Once she was the only woman in the world allowed to wear this perfume.
L'Interdit. Created by Givenchy for Audrey Hepburn.

Launched in 1948, it is a hysterically sweet bouquet of white flowers with a heady preponderance of tuberose, created by one of the great woman perfumers of the twentieth century, Germaine Cellier.

Cellier went on to create all the fragrances for couturier Pierre Balmain, starting with the modern classic Vent Vert in 1945, which translates, somewhat unfortunately, as 'Green Wind'. This was the first out-and-out 'green' fragrance, with sharp, raw notes of leaves and sap mingled with dewy spring flowers. Revolutionary at the time, it took years for fashion to catch up with Vent Vert, and green fragrances only came into their own in the sporty 1970s. They continue to be popular.

It always helped when launching a new fragrance to whet the public's appetite by first making it exclusively available only to couture clients or even one woman. L'Interdit ('The Forbidden One') was created for Hepburn alone to wear at first, being 'interdit' to others. This link with the gamine actress was exploited when she became the face of the fragrance.

Madame Rochas was launched in 1960 by Hélène Rochas after her husband's death. It is cooler and less sensual than Femme, his tribute to her.

Dior and after

Christian Dior was the designer who galvanized fashion after the War with his dramatically feminine New Look of 1947. He launched his first fragrance, Miss Dior, a spicy floral chypre, at the same time, starting the practice of naming one particular dress after the fragrance of the house each season. The press went wild over the flagrant extravagance of the clothes, an escapist antidote to the hardship most women were experiencing in the aftermath of war. Few could afford the clothes; many, however, could buy the idea of luxury enshrined in the scent bottle. A little flacon of Miss Dior on a dressing-table was a symbol of an otherwise unobtainable lifestyle. Dior was a master at licensing his name to trade on the Diormania that followed the success of the New Look. Not only scents, but hats, furs, shoes and foreign branches of the boutique quickly followed. The *New York Times* called the house of Dior 'the General Motors of the Paris haute couture'.

Roudnitska was commissioned to produce Dior's next perfume, the angelic Diorissimo of 1956. Roudnitska had moved dramatically away from the aesthetics of his previous fragrances which he now rejected as 'candied, gastronomical' and effected a one-man revolution, with a nod to Cellier, in favour of light, pure perfumes. He began to douse his creations in something clean and cold, stripping them of syrupy base notes. They came up light and shivering. Diorissimo is like diaphanous streamers of lily-of-the-valley liberated to float in fresh air. Several hours on, it does not dry down into the synthetic musks and vanillin of most fragrances but still echoes dew-fresh cerulean flowers, above all, the lily-of-the-valley that was Christian Dior's lucky flower.

The original bottle for Miss Dior (*below*) was an amphora shape, echoing the exaggerated nipped-in waist and full skirts of Dior's famous New Look collection of 1947 (*opposite*), which revolutionized post-war fashion.

While most other perfumers had ended up in one of the huge fragrance wholesale companies by this time, Roudnitska had his own company, Art et Parfum, which meant that the royalties from his fragrances accrued to himself alone. His maxim in creating a fragrance was the minimalist 'keep it simple'. 'How can you keep 90 ingredients under control?' he once said to me. 'It's as though a painter were to fling every colour he could think of on to the canvas – the result would be colourless grey.' Diorissimo has a drastically short formula of around 30 ingredients, a masterpiece of minimalism. Roudnitska went on to produce other scents for Dior: the spicy chypre Diorella, Eau Fraîche, and the famous Eau Sauvage of 1966. Continuing in the fresh, airy theme, Eau Sauvage is a masterpiece, based round two new synthetics. It kick-started the men's side of the business, which had languished for decades, and started the fashion for women borrowing men's fragrances. It was the 1960s, and everything had changed. Women no longer wanted to smell like 'women', they wanted to smell young, androgynous, hardly perfumed – the opposite of their mothers with their 'grande dame' 1950s bouquets.

While iconoclastic fragrances like Eau Sauvage did well in the 1960s, perfume as a whole did not. The youth market expanded hugely, but fragrance was not on its shopping list. Ready-to-wear snatched the lead from the couture, and the newest, latest thing became more important than the smartest thing. Fragrance just wasn't rock 'n' roll. And it certainly wasn't feminism. If anything, it was an anachronistic symbol of women's enslavement as the merely decorative sex.

Young Dior-trained couturier Yves Saint Laurent launched his green chypre, Y, in 1964, a bridging effort between the bourgeois chypres of the 1950s and the greener notes of the 1960s. In 1966, Guy Laroche's Fidji, a harmony of exotic blossoms with bright green overtones, captured the *Zeitgeist* more effectively with its lotus-eating island life ads.

The three couturiers who sum up the spirit of the 1960s, André Courrèges, Pierre Cardin and Paco Rabanne, also launched fragrances to capitalize on their enormous publicity, but somewhat after the event. Courrèges launched Empreinte ('Impression') in 1971 and then Eau de Courrèges. Given the futuristic fabulousness of his clothes, he should have been selling rocket fuel as scent, but neither are anything like as forward-thinking as the clothes were. Cardin, famous for licensing his name to sell almost anything, made clothes from vinyl, brooches from nails, and sold his Eau Cardin in a modular space-age bottle.

Paco Rabanne designed in the same radically modern vein. In 1964 he produced twelve experimental dresses in plastic and metal, hewn with pliers

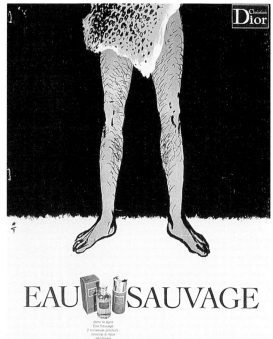

The brilliant commercial artist René Gruau painted all the Dior fragrance ads of the 1950s and 1960s, including the original Miss Dior ad (*opposite*) and the one for Eau Sauvage (*above*).

and a blowtorch instead of needles and scissors. The scandalous collection was the first to be shown on black models who, rather than walking decorously down the catwalk, danced on a podium. His love of metal is reflected in his fragrances. Calandre (French for a car's radiator grille) was launched in 1969. Rabanne had specified the tang of aluminium and steel for the scent, and apparently the first attempt was too successful and had to be reformulated into a more acceptable blend with cypress and lemon. Métal, in 1979, continued the steely modernist theme.

When couturiers first began to launch fragrances, many perfumers worried that they would turn scent into little more than accessories for fashion, and in some ways, they have been right. Nowadays, a fashion designer cannot wait to launch a fragrance as a money-spinning venture that often has very little to do with him and which is calculated purely as an effective marketing exercise. But the answer to the question as to whether fashion or fragrance has won is not so simple. The enormous profits that a fragrance can generate has brought its own power to the perfume companies that contract with a designer to use his name. In some ways, fashion has become an accessory to the fragrance, especially the couture, which is now little more than an expensive publicity exercise to keep the couturier's name current, boosting sales of the perfumes and cosmetics. Fashion designers may have looked to fragrance as a lucrative sideline, but insidiously, it has taken over. What couture is really dressing up is the fragrance itself.

The Advent of the Americans

Throughout the first half of the century, French perfumery dominated the international market and shaped tastes in perfume, but in the 1950s, the French cartel was challenged by the serious entry of the Americans into the business. Until the Second World War American designers mostly worked anonymously for big manufacturers' labels. With the emergence of ready-to-wear as the guiding force of fashion in the 1960s they began to come into their own, and in the 1970s, with Halston's successful fragrance, followed by Calvin Klein's domination in the 1980s, they have put American designer scents firmly on the map. But it was not American designers who first challenged perfume rule from Paris. It was the cosmetic companies.

Elizabeth Arden, who headed a cosmetic empire in the States, had already launched fragrances, including the successful Blue Grass, in the 1930s. Helena Rubinstein, too, had a few, as had their implacable but witty foe, Charles Revson, head of Revlon. Called 'that man' by Arden, he brought out a men's fragrance of the same name to irritate her. But French perfume remained the hallmark of prestige and style. It had history and snobbery behind it. If buying a perfume is about buying a dream, then the American dream did not bottle nearly as well as the Continental version.

In the 1950s, Estée Lauder began to change all this. It wasn't easy. How was a lower middle-class, uneducated girl from Queens, New York, with no backing going to challenge the couturier-scents that wafted in with

After Youth Dew, Estée Lauder got the idea for her next scent at a party: 'I saw the light from two crystal chandeliers shimmering in a glass of champagne. Imagine if I could capture that image in a fragrance, I thought.' The result was Estée, named after herself. Her great rival, Charles Revson, who lived to copy her, came out with a fragrance named after himself, Charlie. At last he had a success to rival Youth Dew.

an aristocratic and fashionable air from Paris? Estée Lauder had launched her cosmetics company with the help of her pharmacist uncle from grassroots beginnings, but by the 1950s her business was well-established and based in Manhattan. She was still small, however, compared with the market leaders Rubinstein, Arden and Revlon. It was at this point that she decided to launch a fragrance.

Until the 1950s, scent was an extremely expensive luxury, much more, relatively, than today. Few women used it every day; most dabbed it discreetly behind their ears on gala occasions only. There was no such thing as a diffusion line for a scent. It came only as extrait or pure perfume. The tradition was that fragrance was a romantic gift from a man to a woman. As late as 1949 the Office Dourdin in Paris issued a market research report revealing that only 18 per cent of

Parisian women (the most advanced in these matters, one would assume) bought their own scent. Mrs Lauder was to change all that with a simple and brilliant strategy. Her Youth Dew, launched in 1952, was not sold as a perfume. As she put it: 'How could I get the American woman to buy her own perfume? I would not call it a perfume. I would call it Youth Dew. A bath oil that doubled as a skin perfume. . . . A woman could buy herself a bottle of bath oil the way she'd buy a lipstick – without feeling guilty, without waiting for her birthday, anniversary, graduation, without giving tiresome hints to her husband. . . . Instead of using their French perfumes by the drop, behind each ear, women were using Youth Dew by the bottle in their bath water. I believe that advances for women got a boost when a woman felt free to dole out some of her own dollars for her own choice of scents.' Feminist firepower or inspired marketing, Youth Dew took America

Elizabeth Arden's Blue Grass of 1936 was a light, sweet floral named for the blue grass country in Kentucky where she bred racehorses at her ranch, Maine Chance.

Youth Dew started a trend of escalating concentrations in perfume. French fragrances have had to to keep up and have gone from an average of 15 per cent perfume oils in the 1920s to around 25 per cent now.

by storm. In 1953, it had a turnover of US $50,000. By 1984, the figure had risen to over US $150 million. Estée Lauder's ascension to the role of Queen of Cosmetics is based on the fragrance.

Youth Dew was also more powerful than French perfumes. It had a higher proportion of perfume oils, setting a trend that culminated in the 1980s with scents so strong that some New York restaurant owners put signs in their windows reading 'Please no wearers of Passion, Giorgio or Poison.'

The American influence didn't just change taste. It also spearheaded a fragrance revolution in line with the sexual one. Until then, most women had one husband – and one fragrance – for life. No longer. Scent now became a case of serial monogamy at least, a rotating stable of scents at most, an idea also credited to Mrs Lauder. 'You wouldn't wear the same dress to play tennis in as you would to a party, why wear the same fragrance?' The 'stable' concept introduced the era where scents detonate on the market like atom bombs, glow brightly in a brief blaze of publicity, and then, mostly, evaporate. Some deplore the new aggressively marketed scents and, like perfumer Edmond Roudnitska, think the fragrance business has lost its dedication to quality and innovation. Others revel in the fact that we have more choice of fragrance than ever before and that scent is worn more liberally, not saved for special occasions. Whichever way you look at it, a scent can no longer be slipped on to the market in the hope that people will like it. A great deal of highly expensive spin is the first stage to selling scent nowadays; the potion in the bottle comes a definite second.

Chapter Five

The Sensual Sell

A modern perfume is a fetish of our culture, an amulet of eroticism and status that we treasure like the reliquaries of saintly bones. The only difference is that, in our consumer era, these relics have designer rather than divine origin. Perfume, someone once said, is 10 per cent scent, 90 per cent spin. Call it what you will – hype, blag, entertainment or a scandal – the fact remains that brilliant marketing is what sells scent. In a marketplace saturated with other people's perfumes, you need to pull off a *tour de force* to get yours on the frontline that is the counter. Selling a perfume today means investing millions of dollars in promotion: packaging, advertising, glamorous parties guaranteeing media coverage, and, for heavily backed thoroughbreds, the 'film of the flacon' in the form of an arthouse TV commercial. If trade is war by other means, then perfume wars are fought tooth and manicured nail.

The Launch Party

'You shall go to the ball, even if another one will have you on your knees,' is the maxim that sums up the life of a magazine beauty editor. The role of a beauty editor is only thirdly and fourthly to be a writer and/or stylist. First and foremost, she must attend launch events for new beauty products as the glamorously dressed embodiment of *Vogue* or *Harper's Bazaar* or *Elle*. Secondly, she has to produce 'mentions' of these new products in her glossy pages. Fashion magazines rely on perfume and beauty advertising above all else for their revenue, and while advertising should be its own reward, all too often it isn't. The companies that advertise in a magazine often expect editorial

Yves Saint Laurent with style guru and former *Vogue* editor Diana Vreeland at the Opium launch.

The era of the mega-launch arrived with a bang at Yves Saint Laurent's party on a junk in Manhattan's East River to launch Opium in 1978. The junk was decked out in oriental splendour and rumours flew that a real opium den was hidden below the hatches.

coverage as well. And a beauty editor is under pressure – albeit silken – from cosmetic company public relations executives to give it. At the same time, she has a duty to tell her readers about products she thinks are truly original.

Selling perfume is about selling something indefinable, invisible and covetable: glamour. A perfume acquires this courtesy of its advertising, its packaging, and its launch. The parties are not new – Rochas held parties to which he invited socially influential people to launch his fragrances in the 1940s – but the modern era of mega-launches is usually dated from Yves Saint Laurent's notorious party for Opium on a Chinese junk on Manhattan's East River in 1978.

The Opium party had all the right ingredients plus that extra something that Saint Laurent has always turned to his advantage: bad publicity. A thousand people were invited, a mix of journalists and Saint Laurent friends who also happened to be celebrities:

Cher, Truman Capote, Paloma Picasso and the Studio 54 crowd – the Beautiful People of the day. Photographers snapped away while Chinese acrobats leapt through the air, the champagne flowed and fireworks spelled out the YSL logo over New York at a estimated cost of US $30,000 a minute, while rumour had it that – scandalously – a real opium den was secreted in the hold, complete with rafts of velvet cushions and hookah pipes. True or not, this could only fuel the aura of dangerous allure that hung over the perfume, already gaining column inches because of its name.

It was a huge risk. Yes, it was chic, but would they get it in Des Moines? The publicity the party generated coupled with the massive advertising campaign worked. The Opium launch created that vacuum of desire that every perfume aims to fill. People wanted a forbidden taste of the elixir of decadence it represented. And they could get it – for around US $50 at Bullock's. The party made Yves Saint Laurent a name in Middle America.

The Opium launch was good, but how does it compare with the extravaganza for Dior's Dune in 1992, a spectacular celebration that carried Dior on to the French stock exchange? Dior's president, Maurice Roger, invited hundreds of journalists from round the world to a three-day party in Biarritz, completely booking out the grand Hôtel du Palais on the magnificent crescent of Biarritz's beach. The journalists were all flown in on private jets. The entire town – France's most chic resort – was taken over by a tribe of Dune people, all wearing the perfume's peach colour. A fleet of Renault Espaces were hired to take them to – where else? – the dunes. Here marquees were erected,

While two journalists eagerly take notes in the background, socialites and celebrities gather round Yves Saint Laurent to celebrate the launch of Opium: Marina Schiano, who organized the party, leans between Saint Laurent and Nan Kempner to clasp hands with Diana Vreeland.

champagne flowed, a Byzantine feast was piled high, while local Basque cultural activities were demonstrated. Unfortunately, the Dune PR army had failed to notice that this scenic area was adjacent to a nudist beach, and the ambiance of the dunes was lent a gamier flavour by the sight of middle-aged naked Frenchmen trotting back and forth to the surf.

But the party had only just begun. Later that same night, at the Hôtel du Palais, a gala affair was organized. First, lasers speared the sky above the sea, a voice announced the birth of a new perfume, like Venus, from the waves, fireworks exploded, and suddenly, from behind a rock in the ocean, a giant two-storey inflatable Dune bottle shot up out of the water.

Christian Dior's Dune was launched in 1991 to fanfare and fireworks. At one point an inflatable bottle of Dune two storeys high rose out of the sea from behind a rock.

Journalists, flown in from all over the world by Christian Dior, gaze out to sea at the gigantic bottle of Dune that has emerged from the waves.

And there was still more publicity to come. A few weeks later, Dior designer Gianfranco Ferre presided over a lavish ball at the Château-le-Vicomte outside Paris packed with celebrities, aristocrats and, of course, journalists, who were there *en masse* to gauge the glamour-rating of the event and report it to the world.

As Carole Bouquet, the French actress who is the 'face' of No 5 once told me, 'I get treated like a film star by Chanel; no film producer can afford to do that nowadays.' Given that companies like Ralph Lauren have the same turnover as some small countries, it's hardly surprising. The presidents of perfume companies have become like Renaissance princelings or Hollywood moguls vying to outdo one another. Each launch has to be better than the last. For the unveiling of his perfume C'est La Vie!, couturier Christian Lacroix took over L'Opéra Comique in Paris, and a glittering crowd gathered to watch a wonderful spectacle at which Sylvie Guillem, the prima ballerina, danced, Utte Lemper sang, dwarves performed circus acts, and afterwards the Gypsy Kings played live while everyone partied into the small hours. Cost: a reputed three-quarters of a million dollars.

Concorde is the journalists' equivalent of a school bus for these transatlantic events. If it's Monday, it must be the Paris Opéra, filled with 8,000 Casablanca lilies for the relaunch of Yves Saint Laurent's Y. If it's Thursday it must be Manhattan, and the launch of Giorgio Armani's Giò. For this, Armani had a phalanx of workers transform 5,500 sq m (60,000 sq ft) of prime Manhattan real estate into a pasha's palace. Even the furniture flew first class – cushions were jetted in from Milan and brass serving dishes from Morocco – and Whoopi Goldberg, Isabella Rossellini, Cher, Linda Evangelista and Lauren Bacall were transported from the four corners of the planet.

Celebrities are an important draw because they guarantee MMC – More Media Coverage. Dolce & Gabbana had Madonna, Naomi Campbell and every other Italian celebrity at theirs. For Zino, Davidoff had James Brown crooning; for Poème, Lancôme had Jessye Norman and Charles Aznavour serenading, and Juliette Binoche, the French film star who is the 'face' of the fragrance, declaiming Baudelaire. Returning to their hotel rooms afterwards, journalists have to fight through a sea of paper bags full of beauty gifts to fall, exhausted and blasé, on their king-sized beds.

When the thought of another perfume-fuelled party prompts media groans, PRs are wont to try Something Different. Helena Rubinstein launched her Heaven Sent in the 1940s by floating hundreds of blue balloons down Fifth Avenue, each carrying a sample of the fragrance. For the launch of Chanel's Égoïste, a men's fragrance, in 1990, journalists were invited individually to meet an unknown but important person connected with the scent. On arrival at Chanel, they were shown by the PR director into a luxuriously decorated room, redolent with this mystery man's masculine

taste. Leather slippers waited by the fire, oil paintings hung on the walls, a grand old desk was loaded down with vellum books and our host's open diary – but where was our host? The Chanel PR droned on about him for some time, describing his tastes and type, looking a bit hot under the collar. Gradually, it dawned on each journalist that there was no host. This room belonged to a fiction, the 'égoïste' of the fragrance's name. Arrogant by name, arrogant by nature, he had stood them up – permanently. Chanel spent many thousands appointing an interior decorator in every launch country to create this chimera's drawing-room.

Make no mistake, all of this expensive hoopla is there to sell scent to you. Out of a launch budget that may be anything from US $20 to $50 million, an average $1 million for the media launch is a small price to pay. The journalists will communicate the excitement and allure to their readers, the TV cameras will beam it to your living-room. In contrast, just sending round the press release in the mail seems pretty flat. So the party goes on.

The Dune launch in Biarritz was followed by a glamorous ball at a château outside Paris at which Isabelle Adjani was guest of honour, dressed, of course, in Dune colours, as was the cake. Above: Gianfranco Ferre, left, Adjani and Maurice Roger, right, cut the Dune cake.

The Brief

Long before the party starts, a perfume is being groomed for stardom. The real stars of the show, however, are the marketing gurus who craft the image of fragrances like Eau d'Issey and Jean-Paul Gaultier. (Both of those are the work of marketing guru Frenchwoman Chantal Roos.) Marketing gurus understand that perfume occupies a very singular place in modern culture. It is a consumer fetish, a metonym. Dabbing on the perfume is like touching the hem of a YSL couture dress. It's sympathetic magic: wear this and you acquire an aura of that. Jean Kerleo, perfumer for Jean Patou and creator of Sublîme, says 'If a perfume does not make you dream, it is not a great perfume.' He is right, of course, but the dream most of us are buying is not in the bottle, it *is* the bottle – and the launch, the packaging and the advertising.

Perfumes have a front and a back. The 'front' is the fashion designer, who will be associated with its cachet. The 'back' is the perfumer who anonymously creates the '*jus*'. The designer licenses use of his name to a marketing company. From this, he will receive a royalty that could amount to millions every year. In spite of the massive success of Chanel as a fashion house, 60 per cent of its turnover is still due to the perfumes. Some individual perfumes gross around US $100 million a year.

The process begins with the designer deciding to launch a fragrance. Timing

Paloma Picasso's Mon Parfum is one of the rare celebrity fragrances to become an enduring success, perhaps because she is a genuine style icon. The famous photograph in which she stares out of the frame like a beautiful but deadly gorgon was shot by Richard Avedon.

is all. His name will have to be well enough known to support the move. Usually the designer – or celebrity or whoever is fronting the fragrance – gives a brief to the marketing director, who passes it on to several competing fragrance and flavour companies. For example, it would be normal for IFF, Firmenich and Florasynth all to be given the brief for a new designer fragrance. A team within each company may work on the '*jus*' for a year or more. Only the winning fragrance earns a cent – the other companies walk away empty-handed. But the one who pulls it off gains hugely, capturing the contract to manufacture the perfume.

Briefs from designers are notoriously vague. Donna Karan wanted the smell of suede, lilies and her husband's neck. Issey Miyake told Chantal Roos he hated all modern fragrances and that the only thing good enough for the modern woman was the 'smell of water'. Or so we are told, anyway. Creating good 'story' for a scent is every bit as important as making a good smell for it. Those who launch a genuinely new kind of fragrance with a fresh new philosophy are taking a huge financial risk. The market may not understand it. This accounts for the enormous number of 'me-too' fragrances which are triggered when a new idea like Giorgio and Poison in the 1980s or New West and Dune in the 1990s proves successful.

The designer's input may be minimal, even non-existent. The important

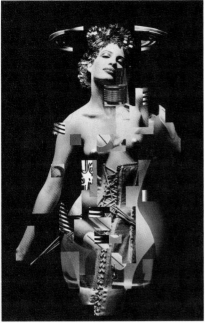

figure is the marketing director who fuses a connection between the image of the designer and the image of the perfume. The stronger the image of the designer, the easier this is.

Of course, it's not just fashion designers who 'front' perfumes – any good brand name will do, including a celebrity. An amazing galaxy of celebrities have cashed in on their cachet this way, mostly with no lasting success. Mikhail Baryshnikov (Misha, in a bottle meant to represent a pirouette), Cher (Uninhibited), Priscilla Presley (Experiences), Herb Alpert (can you believe Listen?) and finally, no less a person than Luciano Pavarotti, whose eponymous scent was launched in 1995. This kind of celebrity scent creates a credibility gap. Surely it's Pavarotti's vocal cords that matter, not his nostrils? Scent is acting here as no more than an upmarket kind of souvenir T-shirt.

The exceptions to the rule are Paloma Picasso and Elizabeth Taylor. Paloma may be the daughter of Pablo Picasso, but

The brief that Jean-Paul Gaultier gave marketing guru Chantal Roos was for a scent that smelt of nail-polish remover and his grandmother's dressing table.

Pavarotti sings – and sells, even scent. Surprisingly, it's good.

she forbids any mention of his name or use of his art at her counters, and, as a jewellery designer, she has created each of the bottles herself and overseen the '*jus*'. Elizabeth Taylor, first with Passion in 1987 and then with her Fragrant Jewels collection in the 1990s, has made a lucrative success of perfume. But then Taylor is beyond being a celebrity – she is herself a hieroglyph of opulence, diamonds, sex and glamour, the last of her kind.

Other brand names have also dipped their toes into the market. Jaguar and Porsche launched fragrances in the 1980s, and in an attempt to reverse the idea that a fragrance must be expensive and denote status, Bic, the biro company, launched a set of scents across Europe in 1988. Sold in small glass phials for an unbelievable US $2.75, they were perfectly fine me-too versions of Poison and Kouros. Just as a Bic biro is a cheap but effective version of, for example, a Sheaffer pen, so Bic perfumes were cheap but effective versions of designer scents. The launch featured the slogan 'Put Paris in your pocket' and cost Bic US $20 million.

Three years later, Baron Marcel Bich, then president of Bic, took out a rueful advertisement in the French newspapers: 'We didn't understand each other. I wanted to be simple. I wanted to be true. But that's not what the eternal feminine was expecting.' John Nelson, spokesman for Bic, blamed the fragrances' failure partly on lack of media hype because 'it wasn't one of those big $20 million launches on the Isle of Mustique or somewhere.' Maybe – or maybe, just like many consumers, the press are smell-blind, able to interpret fragrances only in terms of their marketing.

The Name

Our world is ruled by words and pictures. Scent messages we interpret more simply. A fragrance may say to us 'sexy, sort of oriental' or 'young and joyful', but how do you make it say 'Calvin Klein'? The answer lies in the packaging, the advertising and of course the name.

Sex is a good place to start. Many people wear fragrance particularly when they want to seem attractive to the opposite sex. Romantic names appeal to gentle souls. There have been perfumes called Wedding Ring, Something Blue and Bridal Night, and, more recently, Eternity (Calvin Klein) and True Love (Arden). Marriage for most people might be more accurately summed up by Younghusband's 1936 scent Quickies, but perfume is about fantasy, after all.

Throughout the twentieth century, fragrances have plumbed the darker depths of human sexuality even more successfully. Sex sells, but sinful sex sells even better. Stroking on a sinful scent, you can indulge in *risqué* dreams and still stay respectable. You can look like a good girl on the outside, but hint that you are hot stuff underneath. Kay Daly, who designed many of the advertising campaigns for Revlon in the 1950s and 1960s, described it as giving women 'a little immoral support'. 'There's a little bit of bad in every good woman,' she said. That's the bit that buys fragrance.

Nina Ricci's fragrance Coeur-joie ('Joyful Heart') was one of many named for the festive feeling of victory and relief that pervaded at the end of the Second World War.

Coeur-joie

un parfum de Nina Ricci

Hence women in the 1930s, though probably wedded to one man forever, sprayed themselves with Miss Jezebel, Chute d'un Ange (Fall of An Angel) or Deviltry, launched in 1938 with a red glass Mephistopheles stopper. And forget what happens after a Badedas bath, girls in 1946 knew what wearing Climax, by Blanchard, was leading to . . . if only in their dreams.

The more repressed society was, the kinkier the scents. The first half of the century saw perfumes called Amour en Cage ('Love in a Cage'), Spanking by Schiaparelli and the glorious Coup de Fouet by Caron, which translates as 'Crack of the Whip'. Secrète de Satan, launched in 1930 by Raffy in scarlet crystal, sounds positively diabolical, while Piver's Fétiche of 1926 also hints at the role perfume plays in our society as a consumer fetish.

An entire illicit affair could be conducted through the scent bottle. You may have started out wearing Thou Shalt Not (1945) but relented and become Bachelor's Bait in 1949, then tried Suivez-Moi Jeune Homme ('Follow Me Young Man'), followed by L'Infidèle ('Unfaithful') and finally Liaison. If things did not go well, a woman could then move on to Divorçons ('Let's Get Divorced') launched in the 1930s, followed by Gay Divorcée (1928).

But it's not just sex – any sin will sell. In the 1920s, when smoking was daring, scents were launched called

Tabac Blond, Superfumes and Lady Nicotine. Then in 1940 came the startling Mainliner by Delettrez. The modern equivalent is Yves Saint Laurent's Opium. (Rumour has it that originally Saint Laurent had wanted to call it Hashish, which was considered even more outrageous, because more available.) The advertisement showed Jerry Hall sprawled on glittery cushions, eyes closed, whether on a high of sex, drugs or scent was left ambiguous. The legend read: 'For those who are addicted to Yves Saint Laurent.' As journalist Suzy Menkes wrote at the time: 'Yves Saint Laurent has sent shock waves through the perfume business.' The media went crazy, and sales, naturally, soared.

The American Coalition Against Opium and Drug Abuse and the Federal Justice Department tried to have Opium outlawed on the grounds that it encouraged a permissive attitude towards drugs. In other countries it had to be imported under a pseudonym because of drug import laws and then relabelled once inside the country. But, of course, all this was missing the point entirely. Saint Laurent was not sanctioning shooting up, he was offering suburban alter-egos an acceptable alternative. Opium the perfume is about escape from dreary reality. The name also hints at the powerful narcotic effect that such a scent could have on men who came within its reach.

Poison, which was launched in 1985, took the same theme still further. As the scent psychologist Joachim Mensing explains: 'Both Opium and Poison are feminist fragrances in different ways. Opium symbolizes woman's emancipation through her inner search – something we were very into in the 1970s. Poison is about power in sexual politics. It looks like

OPIUM
pour celles qui s'adonnent à Yves Saint Laurent.

Parfums
YVESSAINTLAURENT

So scandalous was the name of Yves Saint Laurent's new fragrance in 1976 that it was banned in some countries and the scent had to be imported unnamed and labelled once there. The ad features Jerry Hall in a blissful stupor, whether on a high of sex, drugs or scent we don't know. The ad-line reads 'For those who are addicted to Yves Saint Laurent'.

a magic fruit filled with belladonna, and promises the power of witchcraft. It's the female fantasy of sexual domination. He will be passive under your spell, subject to your will.'

Those 1980s dreams of domination and excess have evaporated, however, and no good marketeer would launch a fragrance like that now. In fact, Maurice Roger, President of Parfums Christian Dior, who masterminded both Poison and Dune, the company's gentle, spiritual 1990s launch, came up with the concept for Dune first, but saw that its time was not right. He went on to launch Poison instead, saving Dune for the backlash he knew was coming later.

Wealth follows sex and narcotics as an effective keyword for a scent. Money has always been aphrodisiac in its own way. Hence Frozen Assets, the gold-digger's perfume of 1954. Elizabeth Taylor's White Diamonds and Diamonds and Sapphires of the early 1990s were also aimed at the woman whose values remained skewed towards traditional desires. 'Diamonds have been described as the historical perfume of the rich and powerful,' the press release expounded. To dream of diamonds, it elaborated, is to dream of 'wealth, happiness, success'. The bottles backed up the materialistic dream of the name. Even if you

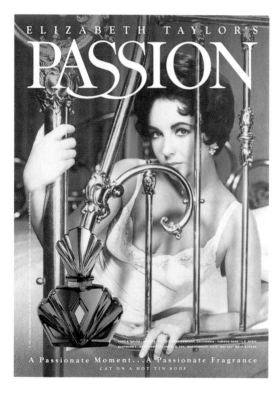

Elizabeth Taylor's Passion plays on the hot-tempered, passionate characters she is famous for portraying. Images from her films are used as advertising to back up the glamorous message. Here she is seen as Maggie in *Cat on a Hot Tin Roof*.

couldn't afford a diamond necklace in the recession, it was a comfort to know that you could probably afford the deluxe edition of the bottle dressed in 'a pavé rhinestone-jewelled collar . . . with three hundred stones'.

But on the whole, both sex and money went out of fashion in the 1990s. People wanted to Escape, get Far Away, and dream about flying to

the Sun, Moon and Stars. Others wanted to retreat all the way back to mother love and be snugged into the womb. The simple escapism of the recession scents led to the foodie smells of what have been referred to as the regression scents, an olfactory form of rebirthing. These have names such as Sweet Indulgence and Vanilla Fields. The last thing that a woman buying one of these fragrances has on her mind is ensnaring a man. They are more a form of self-therapy.

Fragrance names often lose some of their meaning along the way. Poiret's Parfum de ma Marraine, launched during the First World War, translates as 'My Godmother's Perfume', but it had nothing at all to do with godmothers. A 'marraine' was the wartime term for the female penpals who wrote on scented notepaper to homesick young soldiers at the front. In the first third of the century many names were borrowed from popular plays to capitalize on their publicity. The extraordinary bottle for Chu Chin Chow from Bryenne in 1918 suddenly makes sense when you are aware that it was also the name of the longest-running musical of the time in both London and New York. The bottle shows the protagonist of the play in his disguise as a mandarin. The name Amour en Cage was also borrowed from a play, *L'Amour en Cage*. Cadolle Frères, who launched the fragrance, also made fine lingerie and claimed to be the inventors of the brassière. They stated that 'amour en cage', which translates as 'love in a cage', in fact describes the female breasts when 'captured' by a brassière.

Sometimes names were made up to echo more resonances, like L'Effleurt de Coty. 'Effleurt' is an invented word that echoes the French words *fleur* (flower), *effleurer* (to brush something

136

was the only one to use letters instead, naming her fragrances A, B, C and D.

Perfumes were also named to commemorate events. Volt, launched by Piver in 1922 in a bottle shaped like a lightbulb, commemorated the arrival of electricity. L'Heure Attendue by Patou (1945) celebrated the end of the war, as did a number of other fragrances. And to celebrate the first explorations of space, Lancôme launched Spoutnik ('Sputnik') in 1959 in an opalescent bottle that formed the smiling face of the moon.

During the Second World War, especially in France, fragrances followed the conflict with a series of coded messages. The perfumer Ciro launched Danger in 1940, and the following year the American company Harriet Hubbard Ayer introduced two perfumes, Malgré Tout and Je Chante ('In Spite of it All' and 'I Sing'), which came in a pair of twinned flacons. In 1941, Pierre Dune created Près du Coeur ('Near the Heart'), dedicated to the women left behind by the menfolk who had gone to war. The bottle had a framed space on one side to hold the photo of an absent lover. By 1943, perfume names described the hopeful state of France: Attente and En Attendant ('Waiting') before 1945 at last brought Libération.

By contrast, many modern fragrances have prosaic names, none more so than Liz Claiborne's Realities. At least Bijan was thought-provoking with his DNA, named after the very stuff of life itself, and sold, appropriately, in a double helix bottle.

lightly), and *effluve* (emanation). At other times, a chic abstraction was chosen. Chanel started a long-running vogue for numbers, especially the number five. Molyneux followed her No 5 with his own, then Alice Choquet called a perfume Le Double Cinq, only to be upstaged by Henri Bendel who launched Cinque, Triple Cinque. Couturier Madeleine Vionnet

Lancôme's Spoutnik celebrated the first space flights and came in a smiling moonface bottle.

The Philosophy

Charlie, named for the owner of Revlon, Charles Revson, was the first feminist fragrance. Like many modern scents, it was also a lifestyle fragrance. Women bought it more to live like Charlie than to look or smell like her. In her pantsuit, Charlie was the vision of the new androgynous woman stepping out to conquer the workplace. While being developed it was code-named Cosmo, for the young, liberated *Cosmopolitan* readers it was aimed at.

Opposite: When Calvin Klein hired Kate Moss to embody his best-selling fragrance Obsession, there were cries of protest at this 'anorexic' and 'paedophile' image (feminists scrawled 'Feed me!' across billboards showing the ads). But the philosophy of the fragrance had simply changed from the gung-ho writhing bodies of rampant 1980s sexuality to a celebration of youth, tenderness and vulnerability. Moss, by the way, was 19 at the time.

Now the world belongs to Charlie
The gorgeous, sexy-young fragrance. By Revlon

Fragrance is an industry built on vapour. And hot air. Nowadays, few fragrances are launched without what is known in the industry as a 'philosophy': a pretentious word for an image or a story. All three words – philosophy, image, story – show how our minds work. Smell is too visceral for us to grasp. To understand the scent we have to give it a rationale. What we are buying when we purchase a perfume is an expensive, if beautifully presented, notion in a potion. As Annette Green of the Fragrance Foundation in New York puts it: 'People are driven by the concept now. It's fragrances that make specific connections to the *Zeitgeist* that sell.'

A fragrance does not have to be new to feel 'now'. Old scents can suddenly seem new again. During the 1960s, sales of Chanel No 5 soared. Its modern image and aldehydic, futuristic

smell expressed the *Zeitgeist* of the decade when men walked on the moon and women wore white plastic boots.

Most trends have a forerunner, and the chypres of the 1980s – Paloma Picasso, Jil Sander III, Lauder's Knowing – were preluded by the phenomenal marketing success of Revlon's Charlie in the 1970s. Charlie was, in a way, the first feminist fragrance. Its philosophy could be summed up as: 'Young, independent woman with places to go is admired by men but never ruled by them.' The name was brilliant: androgynous, but still somehow sexy and girlie. The advertisement featured not a steamy sensual moment but Shelley Hack (later, appropriately, to star in the TV serial *Charlie's Angels*) striding out in trousers, still extraordinary garb for a scent ad. Charlie was a good scent, but more importantly it captured the way women wanted to be, and reflected it back at them. Possessing a bottle of Charlie was like possessing the elusive elixir of women's new-found freedom; wearing it was like wearing a women's lib badge. It instantly became the top-selling mass-market fragrance worldwide.

In the 1980s, this feminist philosophy went further. Scents got 'bigger' and more aggressive. Women used fragrance as olfactory shoulder pads to increase the scent-space around them and make a bigger impression in the male workplace they had begun to infiltrate in numbers. In this way, fragrances had a positive effect on women's confidence. And, in addition, with powerful perfumes they signalled that they were still women, even while

BLUE SEA–a plunge into the deep unknown. A crisp and exhilirating fragrance that projects the ultimate sophistication of a man. Wear BLUE SEA and experience its sensual strength. Relax and be cool.

INTRODUCING
BLUE SEA™
COLOGNE FOR MEN

Available at
Walgreens
DRUG STORES
and other fine retail stores
Not to be confused with our competitor's COOL WATER. Blue Sea™ and Cool Water® are competing products of competing companies.

Davidoff's Cool Water spawned a host of imitators, none more kitsch than Blue Sea. With Blue Sea, instead of an Adonis in the waves, you get a Chippendale lookalike in the sand. Instead of beads of sea-water, he wears rather too much baby oil, and instead of a sensual expression, he sports a self-satisfied smirk. So close (yet so far) is Blue Sea to Cool Water that the ad carries a disclaimer at the bottom.

they might have dressed with that androgynous 1980s silhouette of broad shoulders and narrow hips.

The philosophy of successful 1980s scents envisioned women as predators, whether on the stock exchange or in bed. The commercial for Poison showed a woman stalking the bottle like a panther in heat; Obsession originally featured a model prowling through a sea of male love-slaves, all ensnared by her sensual powers; and scents like Alexis by Joan Collins hinted that you too could be as ruthless and successful as Alexis Carrington, her character in the TV soap *Dynasty*.

That has changed. As scent psychologist Joachim Mensing explains, women in the 1990s feel weighed down by responsibility and recession. The last thing they need is a heavy-duty

sex-and-success fragrance adding to the burden. Instead of olfactory shoulder pads, they need a scent that will lift the weight from their shoulders. Enter the era of scent as therapy, the scent that is for you alone. The first scents to express this tendency were the fresh-air ozone fragrances like New West, Dune and Escape, all with escapist names and philosophies to match.

Escapism for women used to be linked inexorably to romance, but this too has changed. The fragrance 'philosophy' now is about women escaping not so much with men as from them. Instead, women appear blissfully alone (Avon's Far Away) or with babies (Lanvin's Arpège, Elizabeth Arden's Sunflowers, Perry Ellis's 360°) or with animals (the horse in Hermès's Amazone, her pet Maltese dog in Elizabeth Taylor's Fragrant Jewels collection). Marketing experts point out that many modern women see men now as burdens rather than as vehicles of pleasure. Women no longer need a man to bring fulfilment to their lives.

AIDS, too, is often cited by the industry experts as a reason why the philosophies for most modern scents have a New Age, therapeutic approach rather than a sensual one. This is also why foodie fragrances are so popular in the 1990s. Food is the new sensuality, so it is delectable peach, tangerine and watermelon that dominate new fragrances rather than sexy musks and amber. Women are wearing them as a treat, the way you eat dessert.

At the same time, perfume houses are branching out into new markets. Teenagers are courted with scents like Loulou Blue with a 'techno' theme supposed to reflect dance music, and even babies have scents now like Tartine et Chocolat's Ptisenbon ('Little One Smells Good'), marketed by Givenchy. The press release explains,

'Now little ones have their own special fragrance, just like Mummy whom they so love to imitate.'

While wholesome aromas for all the family are a 1990s trend, sex does still get a look in, though in a surprising way. Marie-Hélène Prevot is Marketing Manager at Joël Desgrippes, where fragrance philosophies are designed from the bottle up. She has a word for the 1990s version of sexiness in scent: 'self-eroticism'. 'In the face of the AIDS plague, and all this international strife in the world, people close in on themselves,' she explains. 'We are seeing the introspection of women now, expressed through self-sensuality. It's *péché personelle*. At the beginning it's pure, as with Dune, when she's lying alone on the sand . . . but it leads to "sinful" self-exploration.' Mensing agrees, 'What is important now is that ads show a woman alone, there is no man around. Women are discovering their own body feelings. It's very narcissistic and it's still forbidden.' There's been a similar trend in the philosophy of men's perfumery. In the famous Davidoff Cool Water ads, a hunk lies back in the waves, enjoying his pecs all by himself, like a masculine Venus. It's spawned a host of imitators.

But while sex continues to play and play in one form or another, absolutely the concept of the moment – and, the industry agrees, the future – is aromachology with scents purporting to give you energy, release your stress or stimulate your chakras. Aromachology is a return to the roots of fragrance as a spiritual mood-drug and medicine. The philosophy of fragrance in the 1990s, it seems, has come a long way from Bachelor's Bait.

Intensive marketing isn't always the answer. One of the most successful scents of all time had no help from either perfumer or philosopher. Known

COOL WATER

as Bint el Sudan ('bint' from the old Arabic term for a daughter), it still sells throughout the Middle East and Africa. In every wholesale perfume company's compounding room, there is a vat known as Mille Fleurs or Pot Pourri. Into this go all the mistakes, the incorrectly measured formulae and so on. Each company's smells different, but somehow they always smell wonderful. Shortly after the Second World War, a Middle Eastern businessman visited a London fragrance manufacturer and smelt the Pot Pourri. The manufacturers couldn't believe their luck when he actually ordered some. However, five years later, when they had to reconstitute it from scratch, they were not so thrilled. Bint el Sudan just shows that, finally, there's no knowing what will sell.

Successful launches like Davidoff's Cool Water, a great philosophy married to a sexy ad married to a good fragrance, are frequently followed by 'me-too' fragrances, some just jumping on the bandwagon, others hoping to make people think they are the real thing.

Advertising

Convincing the press that your concept is right is crucial, but then so is advertising. This is what you pay for when you buy a fragrance. It's well known that most of the time the liquid in the bottle costs only a few dollars and the rest is down to the packaging and the advertising. Only food products are advertised more aggressively than fragrances.

The European launch alone of Dior's men's fragrance Fahrenheit cost US $5 million, including US $1.5 million just for placing print advertisements, and US $500,000 to make the commercial. A successful fragrance has to be constantly promoted at least in magazines, and even a world classic like Chanel No 5 is relaunched every five years or so as a reminder that it's still there. It's got to the stage where the marketing companies question

For the two-minute commercial for Dior's men's fragrance Fahrenheit, a boardwalk 100 m (110 yd) long was built in the Australian desert. A second one, built on the other side of Australia, led into the sea.

whether they really want a classic, which will demand constant advertising support. It can be more lucrative to launch a fragrance in a blaze of publicity and then let it die on the battlefield that is the perfume counter, trampled under the jackboots of incoming launches. As Annette Green of the Fragrance Foundation in New York puts it: 'Fragrances have a built-in obsolescence of five years nowdays.'

Although ingenious advertising captures the imagination, many perfume houses rely on keeping it simple with a 'pack shot' in which the bottle dominates the page like a gigantic fetish object. Because it doesn't tell a story, it doesn't rule out any potential purchaser. Just as common, however, is to show the bottle in conjunction with a woman, the 'woman in the bottle'. With this kind of ad, the central idea never changes. We always want the scent we wear to whisper 'this is the real me' to others, and to ourselves. An idealized version maybe, a secret, underlying alter ego, but the woman in the ad is always us. We have to identify with her to want the perfume.

Women choose fragrances as mirrors. They see themselves as Bridget Hall in the Safari ad, or as Kate Moss in Obsession, or Isabella Rossellini in Trésor. And this is why advertisers pay small fortunes for the 'face' of the fragrance. It's every model's aim to be the face of a cosmetic company, most potently expressed in the scent advertisements. A couple of million dollars for 20 days' work a year is a fine salary for looking good – but it's not

just for looking good that these models are being paid a fortune, it's for embodying dreams.

Bigger launches rely not only on print ads but on commercials to generate an image. For the 'film of the flacon', only the best will do. David Lynch did commercials for Yves Saint Laurent's Opium and Armani's Giò, while Martin Scorsese did Armani's Eau Pour Homme. Jean-Paul Goude famously recreated Cannes' Carlton Hotel in Brazil for the extravagant commercial for Chanel's Egoïste. In this, a hundred models open and close the shutters on to their hotel room balconies like demented cuckoos, calling *Egoïste, où es-tu?* ('where are you?') or are shown in close-up crying *'O rage! O désespoir!'* As at the press launch, the hero himself remains an enigma, only his hand cautiously emerging on to the balcony to deposit his bottle of Egoïste – his sexual spoor. It was a huge risk: would men really buy a fragrance called egoist? But the joke paid off.

Expensive and risky it may be, but without good story, a fragrance is firmly on the back shelf. Take Jean Patou's Mille (French for 'a thousand'), a classically beautiful scent that no one had really heard of – that is, until the 1989 commercial by David Bailey, which was banned in some countries. The ad opens as a rich, elegant Parisian woman watches her husband drive off to the office from her window. No sooner is he gone than she is running out in her couture suit. Cut to . . . our heroine ascending in the lift of a seedy building on the wrong side of town. She flings open a door to reveal a young rough diamond lounging on a bed. They fall on the bed, ripping off each other's clothes. Cut to . . . many

Combien de fois ?...

JEAN PATOU
PARIS

The print ad for Jean Patou's Mille is a spin-off from the witty commercial. The ad-line reads: 'How many times?' and the answer, of course, is 'Mille' (1,000).

For the film of the flacon only the best will do. David Lynch was hired for a telephone-number salary to direct the enigmatic commercial for Giorgio Armani's Giò.

exhausting hours later she leaves the building, sees a church, goes in. She walks to the confessional and leans towards the screen. 'Father, I have sinned.' 'How many times, my child?' The answer, of course, is 'Mille'. Cut to . . . a shot of the bottle round which a rosary wraps itself.

The commercial worked because it was witty, like the award-winning commercial shot by Jean-Baptiste Mondino for Jean-Paul Gaultier's signature scent. The Gaultier commercial was considered particularly daring because it shows a group of unconventional women, old, young and shaven-headed, gathered round a table bitching about men. One has a ring through her nose. It's a long way from the classic man-in-tux-meets-woman-in-stilettos scent-selling scenario that has dominated our screens for so long. Surely it alienates the great middle classes? Maybe, but once again, it taps into the *alter ego* for which many women buy their scent.

The Battle

You have a good fragrance, a great name and a brilliant ad campaign, all backed up by millions of dollars. But what you don't necessarily have is success. That still hangs by a thread. In launching a fragrance, timing is all, and it's not just about having a nose for the *Zeitgeist*. Pity Orlane, whose fragrance for men, Derrick, with its ad of a man spraying himself from a bottle in the shape of a jerrycan, was launched at the time that the oil-tanker *Amoco Cadiz* went down. Estée Lauder spun into crisis when its face, British actress Elizabeth Hurley, was tarred with the misdemeanours of her boyfriend, actor Hugh Grant. Suddenly, the name of its perfume, Pleasures, took on a whole new meaning.

The timing was also not good, in a different way, for the launch of couturier Christian Lacroix's C'est la Vie! ('That's Life!') in 1990. Lacroix was the French fashion hero of the 1980s, head of the first new couture house (as opposed to mere ready-to-wear designer) to appear since Yves Saint Laurent in 1962. Bankrolled by the mighty LVMH group which owns Parfums Christian Dior, it was decided to capitalize on his glowing press coverage by launching a fragrance. The launch cost many million dollars, and the bottles duly went out. But there was just one problem. No one bought it. That's life, indeed. It broke two

The ad-line for Saint Laurent's Champagne may read 'The Perfume of Success', but he was forced to change the name as a result of protests by French champagne-growers.

important rules of fine fragrances. The first is limited distribution. In launching a fragrance, it is important to build up an aura of exclusivity, and hence desire, by launching it slowly in only a few upmarket outlets. Lacroix, however, was widely available from the beginning. Parfums Lacroix was gradually forced to reduce the number of doors rather than increase them. Secondly, it was too big too soon. Lacroix was not a name in Middle America, he was only a name to those who read *Vogue*. A massive launch like C'est la Vie's needed a massive name to prop it up and Lacroix wasn't yet it. As Pierre Champfleury, ex-president of Parfums Yves Saint Laurent, explained: 'It took us twenty years to build up the Yves Saint Laurent name. Y, his first fragrance, made no money, Rive Gauche made a little, it was only with Opium that the perfume side finally began to pay off. You have to build the name slowly and carefully.'

Saint Laurent, on the other hand, has been an extraordinary success in modern perfume marketing. His forte is turning bad publicity to good. He first scandalized the world with the launch of his men's fragrance YSL in 1971, by posing nude for the ad, adorned only in his librarian's spectacles. But the scandal only fed sales. Calculated or not, it was memorable. Opium in 1976 scandalized again, and, once again, the scandal boosted sales. Saint Laurent's launch of 1993, Champagne, was certainly not a planned scandal, but once more, the name got up people's noses. Arriving at the launch in Paris, journalists were heckled by a crowd of French champagne-growers smashing bottles of champagne in outrage at Saint Laurent's appropriation of their product's name. Later, journalists were treated to the unprecedented sight of Yves Saint Laurent president Pierre Bergé engaging in fisticuffs with the wine-growers. There's no doubt that it boosted sales, but Saint Laurent lost its European court battle over the name and was obliged by law to change it within a given time limit.

Limited distribution was a technique milked to perfection by Fred and Gale Hayman, who launched the biggest scent success story of the 1980s: Giorgio, the first blockbuster fragrance to have come from somewhere other than Paris or New York. The Haymans started out at a disadvantage as unknown owners of a Beverly Hills boutique in a market dominated by powerful designer names. But they took brilliant advantage of every point in their favour selling it at first only from their Hollywood boutique (useful star connections) and by mail order, building up a huge demand and sense of exclusivity. They fed this by the novel means of scent strips, the first fine fragrance company to use them. When a magazine was opened the distinctive scent of Giorgio wafted out, linking it in the mind with high fashion, luxury and prestige and capitalizing on one of fragrance's well-known effects – association. After their huge success, scent strips became so popular that every magazine reeked of ten different perfumes, and magazines like *Harper's Bazaar* and *Vogue* had to limit the number in each issue.

Depuis 3 ans cette eau de toilette est la mienne. Aujourd'hui elle peut être la vôtre.

YvesSaintLaurent

POUR HOMME

Yves Saint Laurent's forte is scandal turned to advantage. For the launch of his men's fragrance YSL Pour Homme in 1971, still the era of free love, he posed nude. The portrait is so much more beautiful than the boring beefcake torsos that feature in most ads.

But Giorgio is also a cautionary tale of the fragrance wars: Gale and Fred Hayman became multi-millionaires, but ended up in a power struggle and aggressive lawsuit and countersuit for control of the company. Each claimed to have created the fragrance. They badmouthed each other, split acrimoniously, sold Giorgio to Avon for US $165 million and then launched rival fragrances. But neither have recaptured their success – it's just not that easy. Finally, whether a fragrance wins or loses can't be predicted – we're not that programmable yet.

145

Chapter Six

The Scent of Things to Come

S mell is an extraordinary sense, closely linked to the limbic system, seat of our most visceral emotions of love, hate, desire and aggression. It is also powerfully allied to the functions of memory and creativity, and scientists are now using the smelling process as a model to teach artificial intelligence computers how to think creatively. It's only in the last few years that biochemists have begun to crack the mysteries of how we smell, but they are discovering that it may be the most sophisticated sense of all. We may at last be entering an era where this heavily repressed sense will be rehabilitated, liberated and even trained, the way our other senses are, to enhance our lives.

The Mysterious Sense

Modern, civilized man connects with the world primarily through his eyes and ears. For other animals, however, scent is the fountainhead of experience. It is almost impossible for us to imagine the resonant richness of a world mapped by smells, but a few individuals have experienced it through a shift in perception known as hyperosmia. One such was Stephen D, whom the neurologist Oliver Sachs writes about in *The Man Who Mistook His Wife for a Hat*. Having indulged in a bout of drug-taking, he dreamt one night that he was a dog and woke to find himself quivering with the capacity to apprehend the world powerfully through his nose.

'I went into the clinic,' he told Sachs, 'I sniffed like a dog, and in that sniff recognized, before seeing them, the twenty patients who were there. Each had his own olfactory physiognomy, a smell-face, far more vivid and evocative, more redolent, than any sight-face.' He could smell their emotions, whether they were afraid, relaxed or sexually aroused. He could find his way round New York's streets with ease by smell alone. 'It was a world overwhelmingly concrete, of particulars, a world overwhelming in immediacy.'

A medical student, Stephen D had been something of an intellectual before his hyperosmia, but now he found the rationalization process unreal

EAU DE LUBIN

LA REINE
DES
Eaux de Toilette

The sense of smell has the power to suppress the rational, critical neocortex and release the creative dreamy side of the brain.

and difficult, given the intense flood of odours he was continually navigating. With the enhanced sense of smell came what Sachs calls ' a sort of trembling, eager emotion, and a strange nostalgia, as of a lost world, half-forgotten, half-recalled'.

Three weeks later Stephen D's heightened sensitivity evaporated and he found himself back in a smell-pale world that seemed more distant, more abstract and so much harder to grasp. 'I'm glad to be back,' he said, 'but it's a tremendous loss, too. I see now what we give up in being civilized and human. We need the other – the "primitive" – as well.'

Smell and its corollary, taste, are the oldest senses. They guided single-celled organisms through the primeval ocean towards what was useful and away from what was dangerous. The first brain, called the smell-brain or limbic system, evolved from these scent-receptors. In other animals, it remains the most highly developed part of the brain, but what makes humans different is that, with us, it has been vastly overshadowed by the 'thinking cap' or neocortex, which sits over it literally like a cap. The neocortex is the seat of rational thought. It is this that gives us the power to deduce and to criticize. The limbic system, on the other hand, is the seat of the emotions or 'feeling-tone'. It is the centre of the subconscious and imagination as well as 'gut reactions'. Descartes wrote

'Cogito ergo sum' ('I think therefore I am') but 'Olfacio ergo sum' would have been more correct, since all brainpower originates from the ancient sense of smell.

Smell arouses such an emotional reaction because it has a unique, clear pathway directly to the limbic system. Some of the connecting wires from the olfactory bulb do not go via the cortex, as with the other senses, but directly into the limbic system. The limbic system is also closely linked to the hormonal and reproductive systems, giving credence to the ancient belief that there is a connection between the nose and the womb. It controls our most basic drives: hunger, sex and our sense of security. This is why smells are

'There is something indefinable in perfumes that powerfully awakens the memory of the past,' wrote Ramond in *Observations dans les Pyrénées*: 'Nothing so much recalls beloved places, regretted situations . . . I do not know what sweeter moments in my life the flowering lime-tree saw, but I feel keenly that it disturbs long, tranquil fibres, that it rouses from deep slumber memories linked with beautiful days.'

deeply linked to powerful emotions like sexual arousal, fear, repulsion, aggression and nostalgia.

Memory, too, has its seat in the limbic system. 'Scents are surer than sounds or sights/ To make your heartstrings crack' wrote Kipling. Smells have a unique ability to access the gates at the beginning of the trail of nerve synapses that make up a memory. This is why smells can bring back memories with more emotional force than any other sense. A photograph can remind you of a lost person, but a perfume almost seems to bring the person back to life. As the eighth-century writer Po Chu put it: 'It is evening, it is raining. In the deserted house/ (she left me a year ago)/ While

tidying a chest of dressing-gowns –
suddenly from one of them/ With red
hibiscus flowers on it/ Comes her own
personal scent of magnolia/ And there
she is again in my arms/ Caressing me
with that sweet fragrance/ And
repeating the words of love from the
past/ It rains harder, it is cold/ I try to
sleep on the wave of her scent/ That
brought her back to life with me for a
few brief moments.'

Rousseau called smell 'the sense of
the imagination', something many
writers throughout history have been
aware of. Smell works through
association, freeing the faculty of
lateral, creative thinking, and
suppressing the critical, editing
faculties of the neocortex or rational
brain. This is precisely the part of the
mind artists draw on. The fourteenth-
century Persian poet Hafiz wrote: 'I do
not feel like writing verses;/ But as I
light my perfume-burner/ With myrrh,

While our olfactory
nerves cover 5cm^2
($^3/_4$ sq in), sharks have
a huge 2.2m^2 (24 sq ft)
of them. Their sense of
smell, therefore, is
hundreds of times more
sensitive than ours.

jasmine and incense,/ They suddenly
burgeon from the heart, like flowers
in a garden.'

Sight and sound are physical senses;
they respond to the physical stimuli of
light and sound waves. But smell and
taste are the chemical senses.
Molecules have to actually enter our
bodies through our noses for us to
smell things. When you smell
something, be it a pine forest or your
mother's skin, you are taking a minute
amount of it inside you. This makes
smell a much more intimate sense than
sight or sound.

Let's say you are walking through a
pine forest, inhaling that pure, cool air.
What happens is that some of the pine
tree is volatile enough to vapourize and
float free in the air. As you breathe in,
these pine molecules are sucked into
your nose and wafted to the nasal
cavity at the back of the nostrils,
behind the bridge of the nose. When

you chew something, odour molecules are pushed up another passage at the back of the mouth to the same nasal cavity so that food can be thoroughly smelt as well. Ninety per cent of the taste of food is, in fact, down to smell.

Here in the nasal cavity is the scent receptor site, composed of a special membrane of neurons or nerve cells covered in a yellow-brown mucus. This membrane is called the olfactory epithelium. For us to smell something, it must reach this membrane, which is why we can't smell anything when a cold blocks it up. In humans its total area is about 5 cm² (¾ sq in). Dogs have an olfactory epithelium twelve times bigger than ours, sharks have 2.2 m² (24 sq ft) of it, while in rabbits the area equals the skin surface of their entire bodies.

Nevertheless, we are better at smelling than we give ourselves credit for, and the story of Stephen D indicates that we could smell even more vividly if only we could access more of the smell-processing parts of our brain. There are some smells we can detect at 1 part per trillion, like the green smell of vegetables – a primary food source. We can detect methyl mercaptan at ¹⁄₄₀₀ billionth of a gram per litre of air. This is the chemical mixed into odourless natural gas to help us detect a leak. It is also the chemical that gives the characteristic odour to rotting flesh, probably the reason why we are so sensitive to it. Even more remarkable was the result of recent experiments at the Monell Chemical Senses Center in Philadelphia which showed that humans can detect by smell alone the difference between two identical mice that differed from each other only by one set of genes. Clearly, we can smell with some splendour, but for some reason, we don't bother.

Foxes and dogs smell twelve times better than we do and as a result, perceive the world in a totally different way. When medical student Stephen D became hyperosmic due to a bout of drug-taking, he was able to smell as vividly as a dog, recognizing people with one sniff before he saw them, and finding his way round New York by smell alone.

Waving through the mucous membrane like sea-grass at the bottom of the sea are millions of microscopic hairs called cilia. Every neuron in the olfactory epithelium sprouts several of these cilia, which are the nerve endings for gathering smells. These nerve endings are like the brain's furthest outposts into the world, the one place, where, naked, except for a little mucus, the brain itself sticks a periscope up into the outside world and samples it direct. Because these are the only neurons out in the open, they are also the only ones that can die and replace themselves, which they do every month or so. In the hope of learning how to reverse brain damage, scientists are studying how they can do this while those in the neocortex or spinal cord cannot.

The microscopic nerve-hairs or cilia are packed with special receptor proteins. What happens next is still being elucidated, although huge leaps have been made in understanding smell in recent years. Basically, proteins on the receptor cilia bind only with the molecules of certain odours. It's like a highly complex jigsaw puzzle. Each receptor protein has a particular shape so that only matching pieces of the

smell puzzle can fit into it. Smell X can waft over receptor proteins A, B, C and D, but only when it finds Receptor X, with the right shape, will it lock into it and start the process that allows it to be smelt. When all X-shaped sites are filled, we temporarily lose the ability to smell X, until enough of the X scent molecules are metabolized by the body. This is why we stop smelling a fragrance soon after we apply it.

One prominent theory, now scotched, held that there must be primary odours, like primary colours. Your eyes use only three kinds of receptors, each of which recognizes one primary colour: red, green or blue. From these, you can discriminate a huge palette of colours, all combinations of the three.

Scientists were therefore startled to learn in 1991 that smell, always thought of as the poor cousin to our more advanced senses of sight and sound, is vastly more complex. There are about a thousand different receptor proteins for smell, as opposed to the three receptors for colour. This means that we can potentially distinguish a staggering number of smells, of the order of 10 with 23 zeroes after it. However, we don't have enough neural connections further into the brain to distinguish this number in practice. Evolution sieved out those odours least useful to us as the hominid nose took shape.

When an odorant molecule meets the correct, matching receptor protein on the tiny hairs, the receptor protein itself reacts by changing shape, thus altering the property of the nerve cell. This prompts the cascade of chemical changes, then electrical changes, that are fired back towards the olfactory bulb in the brain, to be registered as a particular smell. This bulb, about the size of a berry, acts as a sorting house for the smell signals on their way further into the brain.

Where once another theory held that we have different receptors for lemon, orange and jasmine, it is now known that say, orange, which is a complex of many odour chemicals, initiates not a single signal, but a specific pattern of signals which may be similar to tangerine, but not exactly. The different odour chemicals in the orange bond with different protein receptors and it is the characteristic pattern of signals this produces that allows you to recognize orange compared with tangerine. It's a bit like Turkish carpets. They all have similar patterns, but each one is subtly different.

This pattern-method allows your nose to approach a completely new smell the way your immune system does a new microbe: by analysing it piecemeal. When attacking a pathogen, the immune system sends out many different antibody proteins, each of which can latch on to one small specific area of the enemy. In the same way, the nose examines a new smell from a multiple of different angles, each receptor clicking with one of its particular chemical signatures, so that the olfactory bulb gradually builds up a picture of its characteristic pattern to be recognized in future as 'smell of new car' or 'smell of plastic toy'.

Olfaction has become a fashionable area of research because so much is still being discovered, particularly with regard to pheromones. The weight of evidence that humans do respond to pheromones is growing. Pheromones are scent-messages produced by an animal in order to have an effect, often sexual, on another individual of the same

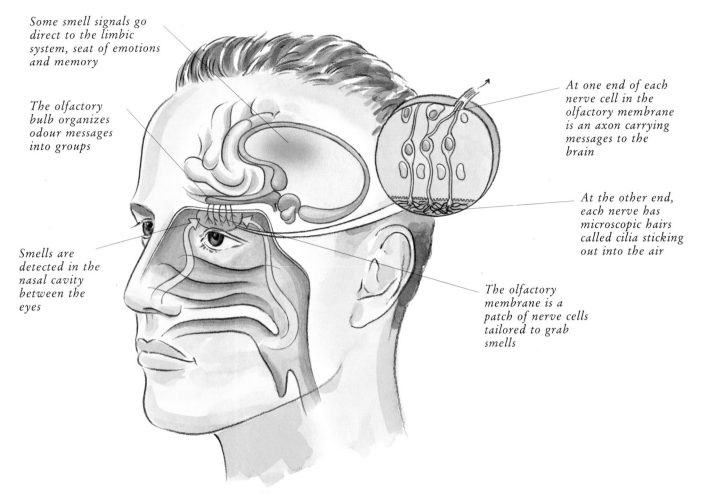

Some smell signals go direct to the limbic system, seat of emotions and memory

The olfactory bulb organizes odour messages into groups

Smells are detected in the nasal cavity between the eyes

At one end of each nerve cell in the olfactory membrane is an axon carrying messages to the brain

At the other end, each nerve has microscopic hairs called cilia sticking out into the air

The olfactory membrane is a patch of nerve cells tailored to grab smells

species. For example, when a sow is sprayed with synthetic androsterone, the pheromone a boar secretes when he wants sex, she adopts the rigid mating position. While we don't 'mindlessly' do the same, it is being proved over and over again that our bodies do communicate chemically with each other, and we do detect pheromones, even when we are not aware that we are smelling them. It is pheromones that guide a baby towards its mother's breast, and it is pheromones that cause women who live or work together to synchronize their periods. Experiments at St Thomas's Hospital in England showed that some human pheromones have a genuinely aphrodisiac effect. When women rubbed vaginal secretions on their chests, it significantly increased the number of sexual advances by their partners in a

month compared with a control group. Smell underlies many unconscious decisions. Some scientists have even suggested that we are attracted to mates who have a body smell that reminds us of the odour of our first love, our mother. Others suggest that older couples could revive their sexual appetites with doses of sexual pheromones, which we produce less of naturally as we age.

Certainly, it now seems that human life itself may depend on smell. Receptor proteins found otherwise only in the olfactory epithelium have also been found in sperm, leading to the theory that sperm use a primitive sense of smell to guide them through the vast rivers of vaginal fluids towards a fertile egg. Far from being unimportant to civilized man, smell is turning out to be primal and crucial.

Futurescent

Now that we know so much more about how this extraordinary sense of smell works, how will we use it in the future? As computers take over more and more of the cognitive functions of the neocortex, perhaps we will adapt. Freed to focus more on the imaginative powers of the limbic system, we might learn to combine cognitive thinking with unleashing the 'primitive' subconscious as Stephen D suggested after his hyperosmic experience. We

Quasar, launched by J. del Pozo in 1995, uses cosmic imagery to symbolize the next millennium. It also contains cutting-edge ingredients: green banana peel and, bizarrely, 'the modern aroma inspired by the headspace of newspaper'.

could learn to do this through harnessing the full potential of our sense of smell.

Certainly we know the brain does adapt to new sensory stimuli. Virtual reality, for example, can lead to brain disorientation known as cybersickness, which is prevalent in the military where virtual reality is used to simulate battle scenarios. While a pilot's inner ear is telling him that he is sitting still at a computer screen, virtual reality may be telling him that he is whizzing through the stratosphere upside down being shot at by Mekons. The brain, confused, acts at first as though it has literally 'lost its senses', but over time it adapts, coping with the contradictory evidence by forging new routes for electrical signals and ignoring the information from the inner ear, literally changing the way it thinks, for better or worse. (Imagine a future where we were so adapted to virtual reality that we couldn't balance our bodies in the real one.)

'In a more positive way, we could retrain ourselves in smell,' says Steve Laczynski, Director of Fragrance Development, Estée Lauder Worldwide. 'With smell we could learn to unlock storehouses of brainpower that could change the whole way we perceive reality in the future.' Just as the ancients used incenses to alter their consciousness, so Laczynski does not think it far-fetched to assume we could use our sense of smell to help us evolve our consciousness in the future.

Already, scientists are using the way we smell as a model to teach computers how to think creatively in artificial intelligence experiments. Until recently, they used vision as a model for how we interpret the world, but it was proving too simplistic. When we interpret the world through sight, we register the shape of an object plus its location, using precise rules. As a model, this method can teach a computer to follow rules, but it cannot teach it how to think.

Smell, however, is not precise. You can't give a smell a location, so instead, you are forced to create an association. For example, smell of Miss Dior = mother; smell of pine disinfectant = bathroom. This is why smell travels through the limbic system, seat of memory and emotion; because we need these to help us label smells. Every time we smell something new, our brains use memory and imagination to help us interpret it using feedback loops; complicated, but creative. Smell forces us to think.

One researcher at the University of California, Dr Gary Lynch, suggests this story: the ancestors of mammals developed brains with an ability to discriminate smells so they could hunt in the dark. They did so by building feedback loop circuits in the brain that allowed them to associate smells with other things. First, a rabbit, for example, trains the smell-circuit to associate a musky smell with the sight of a fox. Then, the circuit will fire when the smell alone is perceived because it will set off the thought 'fox'. Finally, it can use the same circuit to call up the idea of a fox without any outside stimulus. The rabbit – or whatever evolution has turned it into by now – has learned how to imagine. According to this theory, our higher brains are basically converted smell-machines.

Fragrance houses are responding to youth culture's preoccupation with futuristic themes: Rochas's Byzantine is the first fragrance to have a laser-disc label, 'to evoke the techno-age', and symbolizing the sun. It almost looks like an ancient Egyptian artefact dedicated to Ra, their sun-god.

The increased scientific interest in olfaction has happened just as we have become more interested in aromatherapy and aromachology, therapies that use essential oils and scents to calm, stimulate or heal.

The Fragrance Foundation in New York has funded a number of academic studies that have looked into the connection between smell and stress, for example. Inhaling the smell of spiced apples has been found to calm anxiety, and create 'relaxed' brainwave patterns. This kind of research is already having an effect on commercial perfumes. We are returning to a more holistic approach to scents, like that fostered by the ancients. Instead of just launching scents to be sexually alluring, some companies are already creating them for their soothing or stimulating properties. It was research done by the Fragrance Foundation on the de-stressing capabilities of vanilla that led Coty to launch Vanilla Fields, with its huge proportion of vanilla.

While most people assume that smell therapies like these work psychologically, research suggests they may work exactly like drugs, just as the ancients believed. One group of olfactory receptor proteins are identical to those that bind the tranquillizers Valium and Librium, for example. These didn't evolve over millions of years so they could be around to bind Valium when it was invented. Instead, they are probably there to bind natural odour-chemicals which have similar effects on our brains.

The 1990s' yen for alternative medicine has made us receptive to the concept of mind-enhancing perfumes, and alternative companies like Aveda take this even further with scents like Motivation and Creative. These scents

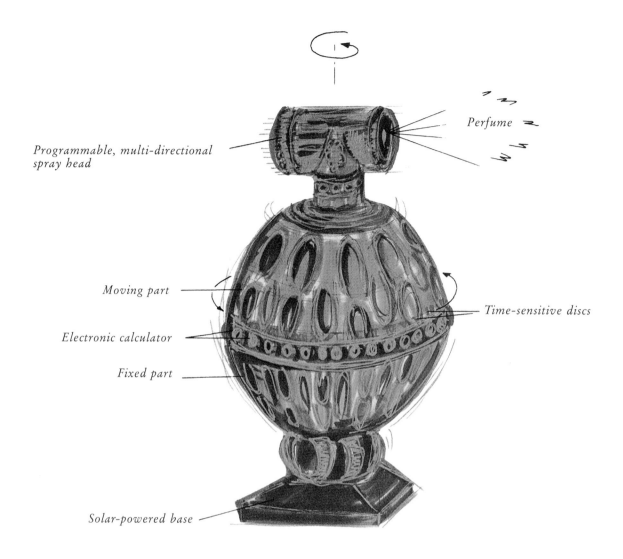

Programmable, multi-directional spray head

Perfume

Moving part

Time-sensitive discs

Electronic calculator

Fixed part

Solar-powered base

purport to stimulate specific chakras (yogic energy points in the body) and improve your aura rather than your sexual allure. Aveda also claim that their scents contain no synthetics, marketing them not as perfumes but as 'pure-fumes'. Fragrances such as these are the 1990s equivalent of a visit to the Mahesh Maharishi Yogi: healthy and holy.

Taking the mystical/healthy theme further are fragrances like Comme des Garçons, launched by Japanese fashion designer Rei Kawakubo, which has an avant-garde philosophy based on health, drugs and ancient Indian principles of Ayurveda. 'Comme des Garçons is a perfume that works like Ayurvedic medicine and behaves like a

A fantasy perfume bottle design for the year 2000 by Rochas. A solar-powered base works an electronic calculator which releases exactly the right quantity of scent at programmable times.

drug,' export director Adrian Joffe told me. 'Rei Kawakubo wanted it to be a stimulant, a healthy substitute for coffee that raises the spirits and gives you energy. It's pure aromachology.'

If aromachology is a return to the roots of fragrance as a spiritual mood-drug and medicine, then it still has some way to go. So much of how we react to smells is based on individual associations, and this personal aspect can alter the physiological and psychological effect of different scents for different people. Nevertheless, some fragrances have been scientifically shown to have beneficial effects. Many have an ability to 'ground' the brain, soothing an excited person and uplifting a depressed person, returning both types to a balanced homeostasis. According to Laczynski, it is likely we will see a 'plant Prozac' in the next twenty years, which, by bypassing the digestive system and going straight to the brain through the nose, will be instantaneous, with potentially few side-effects.

Already, Japanese corporations like Shimizu are commercializing aromachological products as mild brain-drugs. Their Arománity fragrancing system is piped into a building's air-conditioning ducts and programmed to release stimulating or relaxing aromas at set times. Lemon, for example, was found to significantly decrease the errors of keyboard operators. Others allow staff to feel refreshed and work longer hours.

In addition, perfume companies are hinting at a revolution in how we apply fragrance. The next ten years may see the introduction of the Scent Patch, similar to a nicotine patch. Using an encapsulation process like those employed in magazine scent strips and a tiny microchip, it could be programmed to release scent when you want it to without you having to think about reapplying it. Other innovations are less attractive. Surely we can live without one company's Sniff-T panties, impregnated with a selection of odours, including, strangely, pizza?

Our individual body odours are the basis for new methods of helping the police to track down criminals. In the nineteenth century, a scientist named Barruel claimed to have discovered a scientific method of recognizing criminals by 'smell prints' taken from their blood, long before fingerprinting was in use. He offered his system to the police but they dismissed the idea.

Now, police in Holland use Body Odour Imaging to do just that. They have found that the odour-print of each individual is a surer means of identification even than fingerprinting, and, while a criminal can falsify his fingerprints, he can't change his underlying genetically programmed odour-image. It has even been proposed that Body Odour Imaging may eventually do away with the need for credit cards. Your vestigial personal aroma could serve instead: the ID card that no one could ever steal.

One advance in perfumery that is almost sure to come is unappealing. By the year 2020, fields of roses and jasmine may be totally replaced by laboratory-generated essential oils that are odour-identical to the real thing. Instead of being produced by flowers, they would be produced by cloned flower-oil cells in test tubes. Already the pharmaceutical industry is using biotechnology to produce drugs in this way. They can make cells in a culture produce whatever drug they want and then excrete it, ready for use. It is almost sure to have a trickledown effect into fragrance. This method would ensure a consistent, highly economic source of natural oils that is not subject to the vagaries of nature. It paints a stark vision of cyberscent, however, that I for one find deeply depressing. Hopefully, side by side with this alien world of lab-rose and test-tube tuberose will come more companies like Aveda that are proud to use nature's oils, come good harvest or bad.

Index

Page numbers in *italics* refer to illustrations

Index

Index

Picture Acknowledgements

Advertising Agency: 101 (top), 116 (bttm), 135

Beechey Morgan Associates: 100 (bttm)

The Bridgeman Art Library: 8, 9, 76; By Courtesy of the Board of Trustees of the Victoria and Albert Museum: 69; Freud Museum: 71

Sally Blake (photography by Amanda Heywood): 67, 84 (top), 87 (top), 113 (bttm), 134

J. L. Charmet: 1, 2, 7, 12, 18, 19, 21, 22, 25, 52, 109, 117

Chanel: 39, 83, 93 (centre left), 106, 108; /Cyril Le Tourneur: 29 (top), 30 (both), 31, 33, 36 (both), 38 (top), 42 (both), 54, 58, 64 (bttm), 149; /Charles Dolfi-Michel: 34 (bttm); © Sygma: 111

Creative Services Inc: 141

Bruce Coleman: /Nigel Blake: 38 (bttm); /Michael Freeman: 37 (bttm), 47 (both), 51 (bttm), 53

Comité Français du Parfum: 20, 62, 77, 78, 79 (top), 80 (bttm), 81, 82 (top), 85 (bttm), 102, (top), 103 (top), 105 (top & bttm right), 148; /A. Benainous: 86, 102 (bttm)

Deborah International Beauty/Richard Marchisotto: 140

Christian Dior: 82 (bttm), 120, 121, 122, 123, 130 (both), 131, 142; /A. Benainous: 65 (top)

Drom: 68 (both), 70, 73, 75 (bttm), 101 (bttm), 104, 105 (bttm left), 107, 114 (both), 116 (top)

Mary Evans Picture Library: 14, 15 (bttm), 32 (top)

F.I.P.: 44

F.L.P.A. /L. Lee Rue: 50

Fairchild Publications: 128 (both), 129

Werner Foreman Archive: 13, 16, 17

Sydney Francis: 10, 11

Givaudan-Roure: 74, 75 (top)

Parfums Givenchy: 118 (top), 119 (top)

Kenneth Green Associates: 84 (bttm)

Guerlain: 23, 37 (top), 45, 46 (bttm), 49 (bttm), 63, 64 (top), 90 (top right and left), 94, 95 (both), 96 (both), 97, 98 (both), 99 (both)

Robert Harding: 28, 147; /Gerald Hobeman: 59

Amanda Heywood: 67, 80 (top), 84 (top), 87 (top), 88 (both), 89 (top left), 90 (bttm), 91, 113 (bttm), 119 (bttm), 134

Noelle Hoeppe: 32 (bttm), 34 (top), 35, 89 (top right)

Hulton Deustch: 100 (top), 103 (bttm)

The Kobal Collection: 110

Lalique: 78 (bttm), 89 (bttm), 112 (bttm)

Lanvin: 85 (top), 112 (top), 113 (top)

Lancôme: 137

Esteé Lauder: 124, 125 (bttm)

Derek Lomas: 60

Molinard: 24, 29 (bttm),

Chris Moore: 93 (top left *Dolce & Gabbana*), 93 (top right & bttm right *Christian Dior*), 93 (bttm left *Yves Saint Laurent*)

Oxford Scientific Films /Alistair Shay: 2; /Doug Allan: 46 (top); /Howard Hall: 49 (top)

Patou: 65 (bttm), 115

Pilkington Glass Museum: 71 (top)

Planet Earth Pictures: /Rod Salm: 43, /Jonathan Scott: 51 (top), /Carl Rossler: 150, /Brian Kenney: 151

PR Workshop: 87 (bttm), 118 (bttm)

Quest International: 55

Revlon (Creative Workshop): 138

Riverhouse: /Prestige & Collections, David Lynch: 143

Rochas: 155, /[artist's name]:156

Shiseido Company Ltd.: 15 (top)

Javier Valhonrat & Juan Gatti: 154

The Wedgewood Museum: 72

Pages 40-1: from top left, anti-clockwise – Chanel, Cyril Le Tourneur; Chanel, Cyril Le Tourneur; Guerlain; Chanel, Cyril Le Tourneur; Chanel, Cyril Le Tourneur; Chanel, Cyril Le Tourneur; Guerlain; Photos Horticultural; Chanel, Cyril Le Tourneur; Chanel, Cyril Le Tourneur; Heather Angel; Bruce Coleman, Eric Crichton; Chanel, Cyril Le Tourneur; Heather Angel; Oxford Scientific Films, Deni Brown.